ABSOLUTE SCIENCE

Pupil Book

3

Collins

Brian Arnold • George ones • Emma Poole

Contents

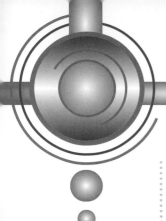

1 Fit and healthy

Professional sportspeople have to keep very **fit**.

A weightlifter needs immensely strong muscles, which can exert a large force very quickly.

A tennis player may have to run, change direction quickly and put tremendous force into hitting a ball for more than three hours at a time.

Even a sprinter, who may only have to run for a total of 10 s, needs to be outstandingly fit if she is to do it better than her competitors.

To keep themselves fit, people who take part in competitive sports train regularly. Their training programme is designed to help their lungs, heart and muscles to work really efficiently, and to strengthen their skeleton and keep their joints flexible. They eat a carefully planned diet, to provide them with exactly the right balance of nutrients they need.

Even if you do not intend to take up a sport professionally, it is still important to keep reasonably fit. Being fit makes it easier to do almost everything that you like doing. It also lessens the risk of having illnesses such as heart disease when you get older. It just makes you feel better about yourself.

What does it mean to be fit?

YOU MAY BE ABLE TO DO WORKSHEET A1, 'HOW FIT ARE YOU?'.

If you are a sportsperson, being fit means that you can play your sport really well and really hard, and maybe keep going for a long period of time.

Imagine a tennis player in a long match. As he moves around on the court, his **muscles** are working hard. All his movements are produced by **contraction** of his muscles. 'Contract' means 'get shorter'. Muscles use a lot of energy when they contract.

The energy that his muscles use comes from **respiration**. Inside his muscle cells, glucose is combined with oxygen. As the glucose reacts, the chemical potential energy in it is released. It is this energy that the muscles use for contracting.

glucose + oxygen → carbon dioxide + water + energy

So, to be fit, the tennis player's body systems must be extremely good at getting lots of glucose and oxygen to his muscles. You have already learnt quite a bit about how this happens. Try this question to see how much you remember.

1 Make a copy of the flow diagram.

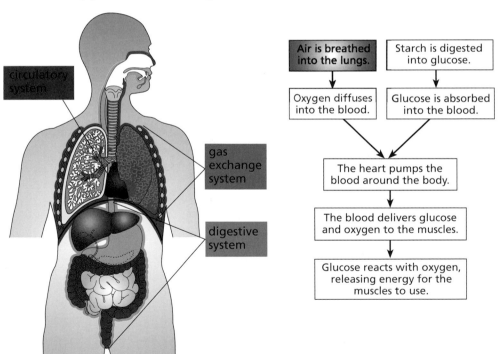

a On your diagram, use the colours of the three systems to show which system is responsible for each step. The first one has been done for you. One box should not be coloured, because it does not directly involve any of these systems.

b Copy these sentences, choosing the correct word to complete each one.

Starch and glucose are both (carbohydrates, proteins, vitamins).

Starch is digested by an enzyme called (amylase, lipase, protease).

Oxygen diffuses into the blood from the (alveoli, bronchi, trachea).

The blood vessels that carry blood away from the heart are called (arteries, capillaries, veins).

The tiny blood vessels that deliver blood to the muscles are called (arteries, capillaries, veins).

The chemical reaction that happens inside muscles, in which glucose is combined with oxygen to release energy, is called (burning, combustion, respiration).

Fitness and the gas exchange system

Your gas exchange system is responsible for getting oxygen into your blood and for disposing of carbon dioxide. The gas exchange system of a fit person is able to move a lot of oxygen into the blood quickly and easily.

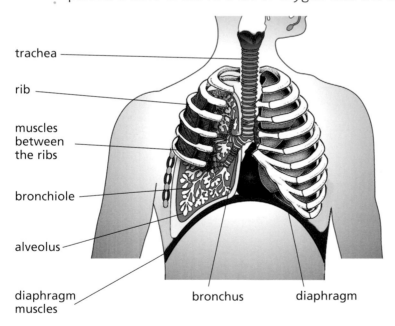

trachea

rib

muscles between the ribs

bronchiole

alveolus

diaphragm muscles

bronchus   diaphragm

This diagram shows the gas exchange system, and also some of the muscles and bones that surround it.

Oxygen diffuses into your blood from the **alveoli** – (singular: alveolus) the microscopic air sacs inside your lungs. Carbon dioxide diffuses out of the blood and into the alveoli. This is called **gas exchange**.

You may be able to do Worksheet A2, 'Breathing'.

It is important to keep a good supply of fresh air with lots of oxygen in your lungs, or gas exchange will not happen properly. The air in your lungs containing extra carbon dioxide must also be moved out. Lungs cannot actually move by themselves – they need help. It is the muscles and bones around your lungs that help to draw air into them, and then push it out again. This is called **breathing**.

These diagrams show how the diaphragm and rib muscles draw air into the lungs.

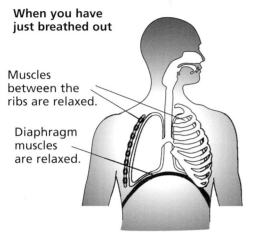

When you have just breathed out

Muscles between the ribs are relaxed.

Diaphragm muscles are relaxed.

When you breathe in

1 Muscles between the ribs contract, moving the ribs up and out.

Diaphragm muscles contract and the diaphragm flattens.

2 Air rushes in because the muscle contraction has increased the volume of the lungs.

To breathe in, you contract the muscles in your diaphragm. This makes the diaphragm flatten, which makes more space inside the chest. At the same time, the muscles between the rib bones also contract. These pull the ribs upwards and outwards, which also makes more room inside the chest. Air rushes into the lungs to fill up the extra space, and the lungs inflate like a pair of balloons.

2 Copy and complete this table to summarise what happens when you breathe in and out.

	Breathing in	Breathing out
Diaphragm muscles	contract	relax
Muscles between the ribs		
Volume of chest		gets smaller

3 Alan and Andrew wanted to find out how big their lungs were. They each breathed out as long and hard as they could into a container of water. These are their results.

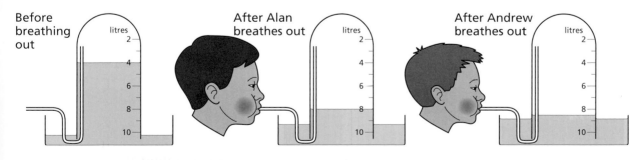

Before breathing out

After Alan breathes out

After Andrew breathes out

a What volume of air did Alan breathe out?
b What volume of air did Andrew breathe out?
c One of the boys plays the tuba. Which one do you think this is? How do you think playing the tuba has affected his lung volume?

Keeping the gas exchange system healthy

Exercising regularly helps to keep your lungs, and the muscles that help with breathing, in good condition and able to work efficiently.

Healthy lungs are filled with millions of tiny alveoli, which have very thin and delicate walls. Oxygen and carbon dioxide diffuse across these walls, into and out of the blood. In healthy lungs, there are as many as 300 million alveoli, with a total surface area of $70 \, m^2$.

You will remember that these thin walls are likely to be damaged by smoking cigarettes, leading to an illness called **emphysema**. The walls lose their stretchiness and get much stiffer. Many of them break, so people with emphysema have great difficulty getting enough oxygen into their blood.

What is in cigarette smoke?

Emphysema is not the only illness caused by smoking. Cigarette smoke contains many different substances, and many of them damage cells.

Cigarette smoke contains

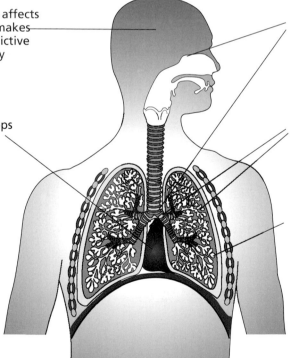

Nicotine – a drug that affects the brain, and which makes cigarette smoking addictive (meaning that it is very difficult to give up)

Carbon monoxide – a poisonous gas that stops the blood carrying oxygen properly

Several different chemicals – they make cancer more likely to occur in various parts of the body

Hot gases – these damage the delicate cells lining the airways

Tar – a dark, sticky substance that can cause cancer in the bronchi and lungs

Carbon particles (bits of soot) – these become trapped inside the lungs and can damage the alveoli

How smoking damages the filter system of the lungs

On the inside of the tubes inside your lungs, there is a layer of very special cells. Two kinds of cells are specialised for cleaning the air before it reaches the alveoli. They make a very efficient filter system.

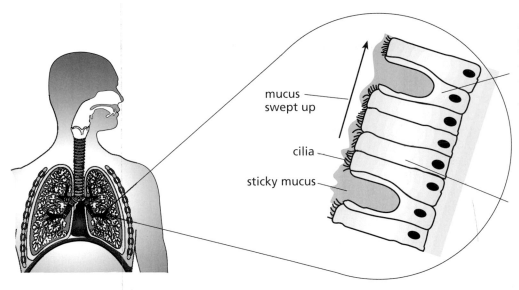

mucus
swept up

cilia

sticky mucus

Goblet cells, make sticky mucus, which forms a thin, slimy covering over the inside of the tubes. Bits of dirt in the air, plus bacteria and maybe viruses too, get stuck on the mucus.

Ciliated cells have tiny, waving 'hairs', called cilia. The cilia beat back and forth rhythmically.

Working together, the cilia sweep the mucus upwards, towards the back of the throat. When it arrives there, you swallow it. The mucus goes down into the stomach where there is quite a lot of hydrochloric acid. The acid destroys the bacteria.

When a person smokes, hot gases containing **carbon monoxide** flow down through the tubes of the lungs. The cilia are damaged and eventually they stop beating. In heavy smokers, the cilia often disappear completely.

The goblet cells respond to the cigarette smoke by making even more **mucus** than usual, though now there are no cilia to sweep this mucus upwards. So the mucus just trickles further down into the lungs, including any bacteria that it has trapped. The mucus collects in the tiny tubes inside the lungs, making the person cough to try to get rid of it. The bacteria often breed happily in the pools of mucus, giving the person a lung infection such as bronchitis.

All of this damage to the filter system can be put right if the smoker stops smoking. It may take a while, but new cells with new cilia will eventually grow.

However, this is not true of emphysema. Once a person has emphysema, they will have it for life.

How nicotine can harm the heart

Nicotine is the **drug** in tobacco and it affects cells in the brain. It is nicotine that makes cigarettes addictive. Many people would like to give up smoking cigarettes, but find it too difficult. They just keep on smoking, even though they know exactly how much it is harming their health.

Nicotine has quite a few different effects on the body. One of these is to make the blood vessels narrower. The blood has to squeeze into a smaller space, and this increases its pressure. So, people who smoke often have **high blood pressure** and this can do serious damage to the heart. This is one reason why smokers are more likely to have heart attacks than non-smokers.

How carbon monoxide can harm a fetus

Carbon monoxide in cigarette smoke reduces the ability of the blood to transport oxygen. This is because the **haemoglobin** – the red substance inside red blood cells – combines more readily with carbon monoxide than with oxygen. The blood of a cigarette smoker often carries only about 80% as much oxygen as the blood of a non-smoker. So, smoking makes a person less fit.

If a pregnant woman smokes, her developing fetus gets less oxygen. This often reduces the rate at which it grows. Babies born to mothers who smoke are, on average, significantly smaller than babies born to non-smoking mothers.

 4 Professional sportspeople almost never smoke. Explain how smoking could reduce their performance.

Fitness and diet

A person needs to eat a balanced diet in order to stay fit and healthy. This diagram summarises the different kinds of nutrients you need in your diet.

Water to keep cytoplasm the right consistency, for cooling you down by sweating, and for dissolving things so they can be transported around the body in the blood

Carbohydrates for energy

Minerals and **vitamins** for strong bones and for helping cells to work

Proteins to make new cells, e.g. muscle cells, and to repair damaged ones

Fats for energy and to make cell membranes

Professional sportspeople eat diets that have been worked out to give them just the right quantity and balance of the different kinds of nutrients. For example, the rower needs plenty of carbohydrates to provide energy, and plenty of protein to help build up muscles. Because she uses a lot of energy, she needs to eat much more food than someone who does not lead an active life.

 5 What happens if a person regularly eats more food than they need? Why is this harmful to health?

Some examples of deficiency diseases

In Britain, most people have enough to eat, but this is not true in some parts of the world. Children in countries where there is famine may not have enough protein in their diet, for example. Even in Britain, people may eat a diet that is lacking in a particular mineral or vitamin. Having a diet that does not provide enough of a particular nutrient can cause illness. The illness is called a **deficiency disease**. 'Deficiency' means 'not enough'.

Anaemia is an illness in which the blood cannot carry oxygen properly. A person with anaemia looks pale, and feels tired all the time. This is because they do not have enough of the substance that makes your red blood cells look red – haemoglobin. Haemoglobin contains iron, so anaemia can result from eating a diet that does not have enough iron in it.

Scurvy is an illness that used to be common in sailors up until the 19th century. It is caused by a lack of **vitamin C**. Vitamin C is needed to help make strong, flexible skin and blood vessels. If someone does not take in enough of it, their skin breaks easily and does not heal properly. Little blood vessels under the skin become damaged and leak blood, which makes dark bruises. If the scurvy becomes really bad, then the person's teeth may fall out. To try to avoid scurvy, sailors used to take limes, which are rich in vitamin C, with them on their voyages. This is why the British were called 'Limeys' by some people.

Rickets is an illness in which the bones do not develop properly. It is usually caused by a lack of **vitamin D** in the diet. Vitamin D is important for helping calcium to be absorbed into the body, and for helping the calcium to be used for making bones. A child with rickets has soft, bendy bones that do not contain enough calcium.

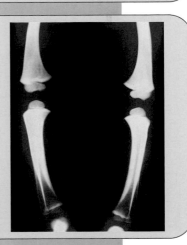

X-ray of the legs of a child with rickets.

Kwashiorkor is an illness in which a growing child does not have enough protein in the diet. The shortage of protein means that cells cannot grow and divide, so the child stays small. Protein is important for making strong muscles, so a child with kwashiorkor has weak, underdeveloped muscles.

You MAY BE ABLE TO DO WORKSHEET A6, 'INVESTIGATING VITAMIN C IN FRUIT JUICE'.

6 Copy and complete this table, which shows information on deficiency diseases. You will probably have to do some research to fill in the last column. The first row has been done for you.

Nutrient	Why we need it	What happens if your diet is deficient	Some foods which are good sources
iron	to make haemoglobin, which carries oxygen in the blood	not enough oxygen is carried, so cells cannot respire and produce enough energy; this causes anaemia	meat, green vegetables, breakfast cereals, chocolate
vitamin C			
vitamin D			
protein			

Drugs

A **drug** is something that changes the way the body works.

Useful drugs

Many drugs help us to stay healthy and fit. Here are some examples.

Antibiotics help to cure bacterial infections inside the body.

Painkillers help to get rid of headaches.

Antihistamines help to ease the symptoms of hay fever.

Can you think of any more?

Drugs we don't need

There are many kinds of drugs that we do not really need, but which some people choose to take.

Some of these do not seem to affect our health. For example, most people drink cola drinks, coffee and tea. These all contain a drug called **caffeine**. Caffeine affects the brain, and can make a person feel more alert. For most people, caffeine does not seem to do any real harm, unless it is taken in very large amounts.

Stimulants and depressants

YOU MAY BE ABLE TO DO WORKSHEET A8, 'THE EFFECT OF CAFFEINE ON REACTION TIME'.

Caffeine is an example of a drug that acts as a **stimulant**. Stimulants can make some parts of your nervous system work faster and more effectively. Caffeine is quite a mild stimulant. However, some stimulants can affect the nervous system so much that they may be dangerous.

Depressants slow down the activities of some parts of the nervous system. **Alcohol** is an example of a depressant.

How alcohol affects the body

Many people choose to drink alcohol, and for most of them it does no harm. For most people, alcohol consumed in small amounts will not cause any health problems.

However, alcohol is a very harmful drug if it is misused. Here are some of the harmful effects that it has on the body.

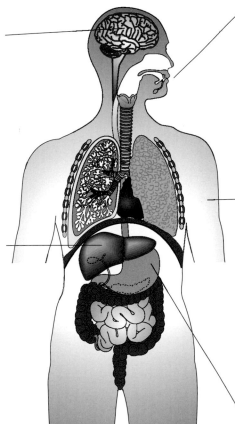

Brain
Alcohol is a depressant. It slows down the rate at which nerve impulses travel. This makes a person's reactions slower. Alcohol stops some parts of the brain working properly, especially the parts which are in control of decision-making. People who have drunk alcohol often lose their inhibitions, and do things that they would not normally do.

Liver
One of the functions of the liver is to destroy harmful substances in the body. This includes breaking down alcohol. Someone who drinks a lot of alcohol puts a great strain on their liver. Each year, about 10 000 people in Britain are admitted to hospital with acute (sudden and dangerous) liver failure. Half of them die. Most of them are young men who have no idea that their drinking has been damaging their livers.

Vomiting
Alcohol is a poison, and the body recognises this. So, if someone drinks a very large amount of alcohol, they will vomit to get rid of it. If this happens when they are unconscious, the vomit can get into their lungs and suffocate them. Quite a number of people die like this each year.

Skin
Alcohol makes the blood capillaries near the surface of the skin get wider, so more blood flows through them, close to the skin surface. In cold weather, this can be dangerous because heat from the warm blood is quickly lost to the air. A person's body temperature can fall much lower than it should be and hypothermia can result.

Stomach
Alcohol can harm the lining of the stomach. People who drink a lot of alcohol increase their risk of developing a stomach ulcer. This is a patch of raw tissue on the inside of the stomach and it hurts. Sometimes, an ulcer breaks right through the stomach wall – this is a very serious condition.

7 Simplify and shorten each label from the diagram on page 13 as a single sentence.

8 This graph shows how drinking alcohol affects the chance of a car driver having an accident.

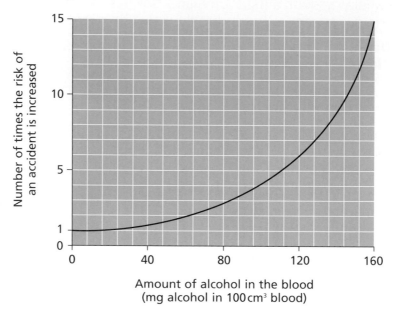

Amount of alcohol in the blood
(mg alcohol in 100 cm³ blood)

a Explain how, after a person has drunk alcohol, the alcohol gets into her blood.

b Describe the relationship between drinking alcohol and the chances of having an accident.

c Using what you know about how alcohol affects the body, explain the reasons for this relationship.

Bones and joints

Humans, like all mammals, have a **skeleton** made of **bones**. Your bones make up your skeleton. Your skeleton supports your body, and also provides firm attachment points for your muscles.

Professional sportspeople undergo training programmes designed to help develop strength in the bones and muscles that are especially important in their sport. This helps to avoid injuries. Even so, many people who take their sports seriously will suffer some kind of sports injury at some time or another.

Bones

Bones are made of a very strong material. Bones are alive – they have living cells inside them that are supplied with oxygen and nutrients by blood vessels. You may be surprised to know that the cells in your bones are constantly breaking the bones down and rebuilding them. If the bones are not used very much, then they are not remade as strongly.

9 In space, the force of gravity is not as strong a force as it is on Earth. Why might this have a harmful effect on an astronaut's bones?

Bones can break. A break in a bone is called a **fracture**. It is unusual for a bone to be broken while playing sport, but it does happen.

Eating a diet that contains plenty of calcium and vitamin D helps to keep bones strong and less likely to break.

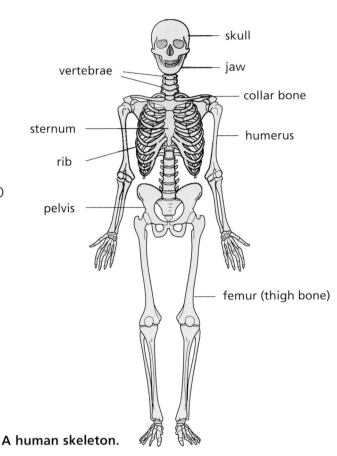

A human skeleton.

10 Which of these bones do you think is most likely to be broken by each of the following sportspeople?

finger bones   collar bone   thigh bone

Ligaments

A place where two bones meet each other is called a **joint**. Bones are held together at joints by **ligaments**.

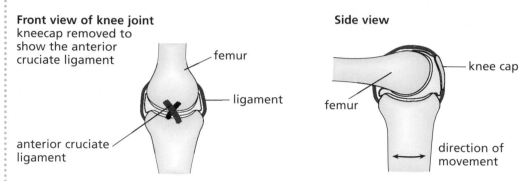

Front view of knee joint
kneecap removed to show the anterior cruciate ligament

femur

ligament

anterior cruciate ligament

Side view

knee cap

femur

direction of movement

Ligaments are extremely strong, and can stretch a little to allow your bones to move at a joint. But, despite their strength, ligaments can still be damaged by a sudden, unexpected pull, especially if they are twisted at the same time. This is called a **sprain**. Sprains are really painful, and people who have sprained an ankle or wrist often think that they must have broken a bone. Holding something cold against the place that hurts can help reduce the pain and the swelling.

Tendons and muscles

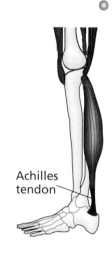

Achilles tendon

Tendons are the strong cords that attach your muscles to your bones. You can feel one of the largest and strongest tendons in your body, your Achilles tendon, at the back of your heel. The strong cords behind your knees are also tendons. Tendons are much less stretchy (elastic) than ligaments. When a muscle contracts (gets shorter) it pulls on its tendon and this pulls on the bone and makes it move.

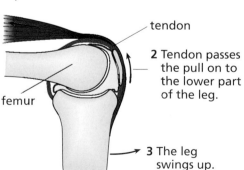

1 Contraction of muscle pulls on the tendon.

tendon

2 Tendon passes the pull on to the lower part of the leg.

femur

3 The leg swings up.

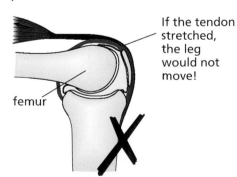

Contraction of muscle pulls on the tendon

If the tendon stretched, the leg would not move!

femur

As with ligaments, tendons and muscles can be damaged if they suddenly and unexpectedly have a very strong pull on them. This kind of injury is called a **strain**, or a pulled muscle. People are most likely to have strains if they do not warm up properly before they start exercising.

A cruciate injury!

Professional footballers must keep very fit. Their regular, hard training sessions keep their muscles, bones, tendons and ligaments strong and ready for action.

Before starting a hard training session, and before a match, a player must warm up. This starts the muscles working gradually. As the muscles begin to work, the heart beats faster and more strongly, delivering more blood to the muscles. The blood vessels supplying the muscles get wider, making it easier for the blood to flow. The joints ease and become more supple. This all helps to reduce the chances of injury.

Even so, injuries during a match are quite common. Knees are especially vulnerable. A sudden unexpected twist can tear the anterior cruciate ligament. This is incredibly painful, and you can actually hear the 'pop' as the ligament breaks. The damaged leg gives way and the player has to be carried off the pitch.

The faster treatment is given, the better is the chance of complete recovery. At a hospital, under local anaesthetic, an arthroscope is used to inspect the damage. This tiny fibre-optic cable can be inserted into the knee, and is attached to a video camera. If this inspection confirms that the ligament is torn, the player will undergo surgery. This, too, can often be done using an arthroscope, which avoids making big cuts in the skin and muscle, and so speeds healing. The surgeon tidies up the broken ends of the ligament and then fastens them together, often using a piece of tendon taken from somewhere else around the knee joint.

Paul Gascoigne sustained an anterior cruciate ligament injury during the 1991 FA Cup Final at Wembley.

The footballer will often be able to leave hospital after a stay of only a night or two, but it is usually at least a year before the injury has healed enough for him to play professionally again.

a Explain the meaning of each of the following words.

vulnerable   ligament   tendon

b An arthroscope is an instrument used to see inside joints.
  i 'Arthro' means 'to do with joints'. Write down at least two other words beginning with 'arthr-', and explain what they mean.
  ii What do you think '-scope' means? Write down at least two other words ending with '-scope' and explain what they mean.
c Explain how 'warming up' can reduce the chances of a footballer suffering from a muscle strain.
d Explain why a person with a torn anterior cruciate ligament cannot walk.

Key ideas

Now that you have completed this chapter, you should know:

- that the circulatory system, digestive system, skeleton and muscles and the gas exchange system all work together to help you to move around
- the word equation for respiration
- how the muscles between the ribs, and the muscles of the diaphragm, help you to breathe in and out
- how ciliated cells and goblet cells are adapted for their functions
- what is contained in cigarette smoke
- how cigarette smoke damages the filter system for the lungs, and the heart, and can also harm a developing fetus
- how data about smoking can be used to draw conclusions about its effects on health
- some examples of deficiency diseases and what causes them
- some examples of drugs and how they affect the body
- the different ways in which drinking a lot of alcohol can harm the body
- how to safely carry out an experiment involving human subjects
- how bones, joints, tendons, ligaments and muscles work together to help you to move.

Key words

alcohol	emphysema	nicotine
alveoli	fitness	respiration
anaemia	fracture	rickets
bones	gas exchange	scurvy
breathing	goblet cell	skeleton
caffeine	haemoglobin	sprain
carbon monoxide	high blood pressure	stimulant
ciliated cell	joint	strain
contraction	kwashiorkor	tendon
deficiency disease	ligament	vitamin C
depressant	mucus	vitamin D
drug	muscles	

End of chapter questions

1 Unjumble these words and match them with their definitions.
aebomoinlgh   mdphgaria   kltnosee   etcinoni   rokshsawokir
oglbte   tedssrpena   nmgileta   icycfedein   Dtvamini
   a A strong cord that holds two bones together at a joint.
   b All the bones in your body.
   c A nutrient that is needed in the diet to prevent rickets.
   d A type of disease caused by a lack of a nutrient in the diet.
   e A type of drug that slows down the working of the nervous system.
   f A large, domed muscle beneath the lungs, which contracts to help
      you to breathe in.
   g The addictive drug in cigarette smoke.
   h A cell that makes mucus to help to keep bacteria out of the lungs.
   i The red substance inside red blood cells, which carries oxygen.
   j An illness caused by a lack of protein in the diet.

2 This table shows the nutrient content in 100 g of five foods.

Food	Energy (kJ)	Protein (g)	Fat (g)	Carbohydrate (g)	Iron (mg)	Calcium (mg)	Vitamin C (mg)	Vitamin D (micrograms)
bread	960	7.8	1.7	50.0	1.7	100	0	0
eggs	630	12.3	10.9	0	2.0	50	0	1.8
chicken	630	23.0	5.0	0	0.8	0	0	0
beef	840	27.0	12.0	0	2.6	0	0	0
cabbage	60	1.7	0	2.0	0.4	40	20	0

   a Name the food that would be best for preventing each of these
      deficiency diseases. In each case, explain your answer.
            kwashiorkor   rickets   scurvy   anaemia
   b Use the data in the table to suggest why chicken is often considered
      to be a better meat to eat than beef, as part of a healthy diet.
   c Which two nutrient types are not in any foods from animals?

3 In January 1998, three young men spent the evening drinking beer.
   One became so drunk that he could not walk. His friends took him
   home and knocked on the door. They left before anyone answered.
   It was a very cold night. In the morning, he was dead.
   a Beer contains alcohol. Explain why alcohol is said to be:
      i a drug   ii a depressant.
   b Using your knowledge of how alcohol affects the body, suggest
      two different explanations of why the young man died.
   c Suggest how this death could have been avoided.

4 Find out about one of the following:
   • the rules that professional athletes have to follow about using drugs
   • the drink-driving laws in different countries
   • the diet of a marathon runner
   • artificial joints.

5 Make a poster with the title 'Keeping fit'.

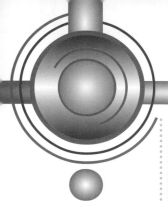

2 Speeding up

This photograph shows a dragster racing car. From a standing start, it can accelerate to a speed of 300 mph (500 km/h) in just $4\frac{1}{2}$ seconds and cover a distance of $\frac{1}{4}$ mile. The car has a very powerful engine that can develop the force needed to deliver this very high acceleration. The designers had to consider the forces the engine had to work against, including air resistance, frictional forces between the tyres and the race-track surface and, of course, the braking force required at the end of the race.

In this chapter we shall be looking at the relationship between the force applied to an object and its movement.

Speed

The **speed** of an object tells us how fast it is moving. We usually measure speed in m/s or km/h.

This sprinter is moving 10 m every second. His speed is 10 m/s.

This racing car would travel 360 km in one hour if it maintained its present speed. Its speed is 360 km/h or 100 m/s.

This aircraft is travelling at 1200 km/h or 330 m/s.

The light from these laser beams is travelling at 300 million m/s.

1 Copy and complete this table.

Motion	Typical speed
a car travelling along a motorway	
someone walking	
a sound wave	
a snail	
a cheetah sprinting	

Measuring speeds

It is possible to measure the speed of some objects directly.

The speed of a car passing this camera is measured using light waves.

This speedometer constantly monitors the speed of the motorbike.

The rate at which the cups of this anemometer spin around is used to measure the speed of the wind.

Calculating speeds

The speed of an object can be calculated from:

- the distance, d, travelled by the object
- the time taken, t, to travel this distance.

The equation relating these quantities is:

$$\text{Speed, } s = \frac{\text{distance travelled, } d}{\text{time taken, } t}$$

It can also be written in a formula triangle:

To calculate the speed of a hiker who travels 1500 m in 500 s, we use:

$$s = \frac{d}{t}$$

$$s = \frac{1500\,\text{m}}{500\,\text{s}} = 3\,\text{m/s}$$

So the hiker's speed is 3 m/s.

YOU MAY BE ABLE TO DO WORKSHEET B1, 'USING THE FORMULA TRIANGLE FOR SPEED'.

As this skier starts and finishes his race he passes through a gate connected to a computer. The computer measures the time the skier has taken to complete the race. Because the length of the course is known, the computer can then instantly calculate the **average speed** of the skier.

2 Explain what is meant by the phrase 'the average speed of the skier'.

3 Calculate the speed of:
  a a car which travels 120 km in 3 h
  b a cyclist who rides 300 m in 15 s
  c a jogger who runs 5 km in 25 min.

4 Calculate the time it takes for:
  a a train travelling at 80 km/h to travel a distance of 680 km
  b a greyhound travelling at 20 m/s to travel a distance of 410 m
  c a tortoise travelling at 1 cm/s to travel a distance of 10 m.

5 Calculate the distance travelled by:
  a a ship travelling at 15 km/h for 24 h
  b a satellite travelling at 3 km/s for 24 h
  c an aircraft travelling at 55 m/s for 1 min.

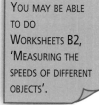

YOU MAY BE ABLE TO DO WORKSHEETS B2, 'MEASURING THE SPEEDS OF DIFFERENT OBJECTS'.

Using graphs to describe the motion of an object

We can show the motion of an object using graphs. The most common of these are:

  • distance–time graphs
  • speed–time graphs.

Distance–time graphs

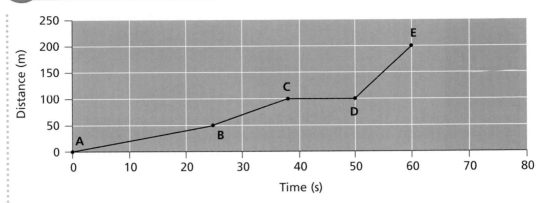

We can describe the journey shown on the distance–time graph like this:

AB: A man walking at a constant speed travels 50 m in 25 s.

BC: He then jogs at a constant speed for another 50 m. He travels this distance in 12.5 s.

CD: He stops for 12.5 s.

DE: He then sprints at a constant speed travelling 100 m in 10 s.

Summary

This distance–time graph shows the movement of three objects: P, Q and R.

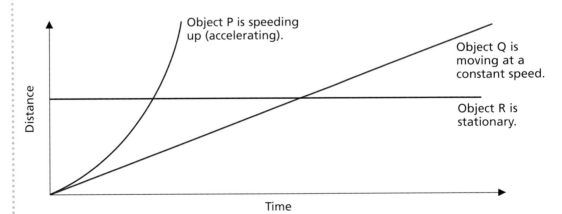

6 Using the data in the table, draw a distance–time graph and write a description of the journey.

Calculate the average speed for this journey.

Time (s)	Distance (m)
0	0
5	20
10	40
15	60
20	60
30	60
35	100
40	140

Speed-time graphs

We can describe the journey shown on the speed–time graph like this:

AB: A car accelerates from rest to a speed of 40 km/h in 10 s.

BC: The car continues at this speed for another 10 s.

CD: The car then accelerates to 80 km/h in 5 s.

DE: The car then decelerates, coming to rest after another 15 s.

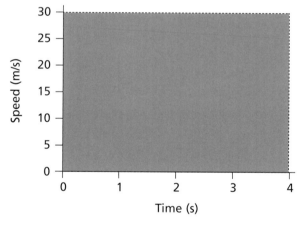

The area under a speed–time graph is a measure of the distance travelled.

Distance travelled = Area under graph
= 30 m/s × 4 s
= 120 m

Summary

This speed–time graph shows the speed of three objects: S, T and U.

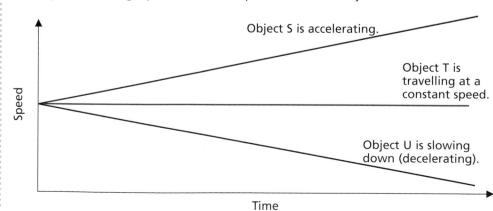

Object S is accelerating.

Object T is travelling at a constant speed.

Object U is slowing down (decelerating).

7 Using the data in the table, draw a speed–time graph and write a description of the journey.

Time (min)	Speed (km/h)
0	0
1	10
2	20
3	20
4	20
5	60
6	60
7	0

Forces and speed

When we apply a force to an object, the force may change the speed or direction in which the object is moving.

Look carefully at these diagrams. What forces are being applied and what effect are they having in each situation?

A force can cause an object to speed up (**accelerate**), slow down (**decelerate**) or change direction. The size of the acceleration depends upon the size of the applied force and the **mass** of the object.

The larger the force, the greater the acceleration.

The larger the mass of an object, the smaller the acceleration.

You may be able to do Worksheet B3, 'Moving without friction'.

This photograph shows a stationary astronaut. In deep space there are no forces acting on him, and so he remains in the same place. To change his position he uses the small rockets on his thruster pack. When he turns these on, he accelerates. When the rockets are turned off, the astronaut continues to move in the same direction and at a constant speed. To slow himself down, he must fire the rockets in the opposite direction.

- If no forces are applied to an object which is not moving, it will remain stationary.
- If no forces are applied to an object which is moving, it will continue to move at the same speed and in the same direction.

8 State how the motion of an object may change when a force is applied to it.

9 Explain why a muscular sprinter may be able to create a greater acceleration than an athlete of the same mass but with a less muscular build.

10 What might happen to the astronaut in the photograph above if his thrusters create too much force when he tries to slow down?

11 Explain why, when two tug-of-war teams of equal strength pull on the rope, it does not move. Suggest three other examples where forces are applied to objects and they do not change speed or direction.

Frictional force or drag

It is very rare that a moving object experiences no forces. An object such as an aeroplane experiences a force that opposes its motion through the air. We call this force **air resistance** or **drag**. If the **propulsive force** from the engines of the aeroplane is greater than the air resistance, the aircraft will accelerate.

propulsive force from engines

air resistance

This aircraft is accelerating.

As the speed of the aircraft increases, so does the air resistance. Eventually the force driving it forward and that opposing it will be balanced, and then the aircraft will travel at a constant speed.

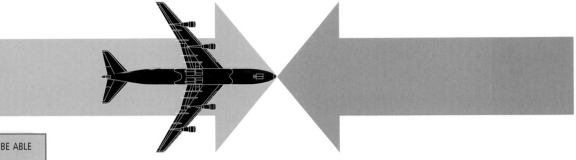

The aircraft is now travelling at constant speed.

YOU MAY BE ABLE TO DO WORKSHEET B4, 'EXPLAINING DRAG USING THE PARTICLE THEORY'.

In order to minimise the resistive force, an aircraft has a shape that allows it to cut through the air. We say that the aircraft is **streamlined**.

Because these objects have streamlined shapes, less energy is needed to keep them moving.

Objects that move through water also experience resistance to their motion and may have a streamlined shape in order to reduce this effect.

12 Explain, using the particle theory, why objects moving through the air experience drag.

13 Give three examples of man-made objects that have been given a streamlined shape so that less energy is needed to keep them moving.

14 Suggest one way in which a driver could reduce the air resistance of her car.

How do parachutes work?

1 The parachutist jumps from the aircraft and begins to accelerate due to the effect of gravity.

2 As her speed increases, so does the frictional force she experiences as she falls through the air.

3 Eventually the accelerating force and the drag force become equal and the parachutist will fall at a constant speed. This speed is known as her **terminal velocity**. Typically, this is approximately 56 m/s (200 km/h) and is much too fast for her to survive a landing at this speed.

4 When she opens her parachute, the drag force now becomes much larger than the force due to gravity, so she decelerates.

5 As she slows down, the drag force becomes less and eventually she will again fall at a constant speed. This speed will be much lower, about 6 m/s (20 km/h) – low enough for her to be able to land safely.

This graph shows the parachutist's speed during her descent.

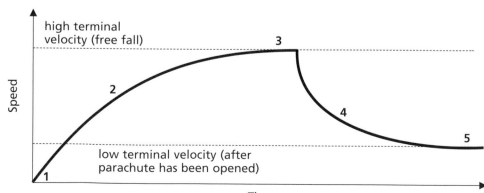

The world land speed record

Men have always had an obsession with speed, whether it is the running of an Athenian marathon, Roman chariot racing or the 100 m Olympic final. Among the most prestigious events in this field have been the attempts on the world land speed record.

It started in 1898 when Count Gaston de Chasseloup-Laubat of Paris attempted to show how well his automobiles worked. He drove his car for a measured kilometre in 57 seconds, at an average speed of 63 km/h (39 mph).

In 1904 Henry Ford decided to prove to the rest of the world that his cars were the best. He drove his Ford Arrow at an average speed of 147 km/h (91 mph) across a frozen lake. He commented later that the drive had frightened him so much that he never again wanted to climb into a racing car.

In 1927 Malcolm Campbell drove the first car specially built for breaking the land speed record. His car, Bluebird, raised the record to 281 km/h (175 mph). By 1935, with the much more powerful Rolls Royce Bluebird, he became the first man to average over 480 km/h (300 mph). Twenty-five years later, the 640 km/h (400 mph) barrier was broken by Mickey Thompson of the USA driving Challenger 1.

From this time onwards, a new set of 'record breakers' made their mark on the land speed record. They drove freewheeling jet-powered or rocket-powered vehicles. They included Craig Breedlove and his Spirit of America (600 mph in 1965), Gary Gabelich and his Blue Flame (622 mph in 1970) and Richard Noble's Thrust 2 (633 mph in 1983). In October 1997, an RAF pilot named Andy Green became the first man to drive his car, Thrust SSC, through the sound barrier, setting a two-way average speed of 763 mph.

Thrust SSC attempting to break the world land speed record at Black Rock Desert in Nevada.

a Draw a table summarising the achievements of the record breakers mentioned in the passage.

b Who was the first person to drive a car faster than the speed of sound?

c Find out who was the first person to travel faster than the speed of sound in an aircraft.

d Prior to the 1960s, all the cars that took part in trying to break the land speed record were traditional wheel-driven cars. What new design of car started to be used during the 1960s?

e Explain why streamlining was very important in the design of these cars.

f What is meant by the phrase 'a two-way average speed of 763 mph'?

Key ideas

Now that you have completed this chapter, you should know:

- how to measure the speed of a moving object in the laboratory
- the relationship between speed, distance and time and how to use it
- how to interpret distance–time graphs and speed–time graphs
- how the application of a force can change the motion of an object
- that objects moving through air or water experience resistance, and that the size of this resistance increases with the speed of the object
- that streamlining can reduce the effect of drag
- how the speed of a falling object changes, and relate this to the forces acting upon it.

Key words

accelerate	mass
air resistance	propulsive force
average speed	speed
decelerate	speed–time graph
distance–time graph	streamlined
drag	terminal velocity

End of chapter questions

1 Rearrange these anagrams and write a description for each.
   a eepsd   e agdr   i liaeerdnmts
   b eeeaartlcc   f tlfcornaii soefcr j daaebnlc ceorsf
   c asms   g eaauprcth
   d rtlcdeeeae   h ltiaermn ioectvyl

2 Calculate the speed of:
   a a woman who cycles 200 m in 40 s
   b a train which travels 640 km in 8 h
   c a racing car which travels 3 km in 1 min.

3 Calculate the distance travelled by:
   a a car travelling with an average speed of 60 km/h for 30 min
   b a sprinter running at 9 m/s for 8 s
   c an aircraft flying at 300 m/s for 30 min.

4 Calculate the time taken for:
   a a motorcyclist to travel 360 km if he has an average speed of 90 km/h
   b a snail to crawl 1 m if it is moving at a speed of 1 mm/s
   c a rocket to travel the distance of 75 million kilometres from Earth to Mars If it is moving at a speed of 30 000 km/h.

5 Sketch a distance–time graph for your journey to school. Label the different parts of the graph AB, BC, etc, and then describe each part of your journey.

6 Sketch the shape of a Grand Prix racing track. If you do not have a picture to copy, make up one of your own. Estimate the speed of a racing car at different parts of the circuit and then sketch a speed–time graph for the car completing one lap of your circuit. **Hint**: The approximate time to complete one lap of most racing circuits is 100 s.

7 Look at this cycling team.
   a Explain why the team ride so close together and in a single line.
   b Describe the forces acting on the team when they are:
      i travelling at a high constant speed
      ii slowing down.

8 Find out:
   a what a wind tunnel is
   b who uses a wind tunnel and why.

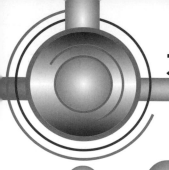

3 Reactions of metals and metal compounds

Titanium

The metal titanium is the ninth most abundant element in the Earth's crust. Like other metals, titanium is shiny and strong. But, unlike most other metals, it has quite a low density. Titanium does not corrode easily and has a very high melting point. All these properties mean that titanium is a very useful material. It can also be mixed with other metals to make titanium alloys – an **alloy** is a mixture of different metals.

The F22 fighter plane.

Aeroplanes, rockets and missiles are often made from titanium or titanium alloys. America's new F22, the Raptor, 'the best fighter plane in the world', is made from a titanium alloy. Can you explain why titanium is used to build the F22?

Why are metals so useful?

These cards show some information about six different elements. You will remember from your studies in Year 8 that elements contain just one type of atom.

Data card

Symbol S
Name Sulfur
State at room temperature Solid
Colour Pale yellow
Comments Sulfur is a brittle solid found near volcanoes and hot springs.
Sulfur does not conduct heat or electricity.
Uses Sulfur can be made into sulfuric acid, which is used in car batteries.
Sulfur is made into fertilisers.
Sulfur is also used in gunpowder and in fireworks.

Data card

Symbol O
Name Oxygen
State at room temperature Gas
Colour Colourless
Comments About 20% of the Earth's atmosphere is oxygen. It is needed for respiration and burning.
As a gas, oxygen does not conduct heat or electricity.
Use Oxygen is used in the manufacture of steel.

Data card

Symbol Fe
Name Iron
State at room temperature Solid
Colour Shiny grey
Comments Iron is found in the haemoglobin of blood.
Iron is a magnetic material.
Iron conducts both heat and electricity well, and is strong.
Uses Iron is made into steel. Steel is used in buildings and to make cars.

Data card
Symbol Cu
Name Copper
State at room temperature Solid
Colour Shiny pink-brown
Comments Copper is an excellent conductor of both heat and electricity.
It can easily be drawn into wires or hammered into shape.
Copper does not react with water.
Uses Copper is made into electrical wires.
Copper is used for water pipes.
It has also been used to make coins.

Data card
Symbol Pb
Name Lead
State at room temperature Solid
Colour Shiny blue-white
Comments Lead is relatively soft and can be bent into shape.
It is very dense and conducts both heat and electricity well.
Lead only reacts with water very slowly.
Use Lead has been used since Roman times in plumbing. Some Roman drains are still in use!

Data card
Symbol C
Name Carbon
State at room temperature Solid
Colours There are two stable forms of carbon: diamond and graphite.
Graphite is shiny black.
Diamonds are colourless.
Comments Most carbon is found in the form of graphite.
Graphite is a soft material which conducts electricity.
Diamond does not conduct electricity and is very hard.
However, diamonds are very brittle and shatter if they are hit.
Uses Graphite is used in pencil 'lead'.
Diamonds are used in jewellery and in drill bits.

Elements can be arranged into two groups: **metals** and **non-metals**.

Metallic elements have certain properties in common. For example, all metals, apart from mercury, are solids at room temperature. They are good conductors of heat and electricity. Metals are shiny and strong.

Non-metallic elements have a range of different properties. For example, at room temperature they are often gases, although one, bromine, is a liquid, and a few are solids. Solid non-metallic elements, such as silicon and phosphorus, are brittle and will shatter if they are hit. Non-metallic elements are poor conductors of heat and electricity, except for carbon, in the form of graphite, which is a good conductor of electricity.

1 For each of the elements shown on the data cards, decide whether it is a metal or a non-metal. Explain how you have come to your decision. The first one is done for you.

Sulfur is a non-metal. It does not conduct heat or electricity and it is brittle.

2 Consider the following statements. Explain, using examples, why each statement is wrong.
   a All non-metallic elements are gases at room temperature.
   b All non-metallic elements are poor conductors of electricity.
   c All metallic elements are solids at room temperature.

3 Using the element data cards, give one use of each metal. Explain why that particular element is suitable for the use you have given.

How do metals react with acids?

When a metal such as zinc is added to dilute **hydrochloric acid**, bubbles can be seen. These bubbles show that a **chemical reaction** is taking place. A new substance, a gas, is being made.

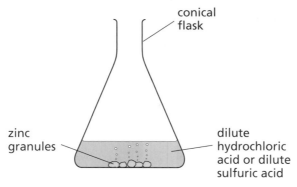

A similar chemical reaction takes place when zinc metal is added to **sulfuric acid**. Again, the bubbles show that a gas is being produced – what gas is being given off?

By looking at the formulas of the two different acids we can discover what they have in common that would make them react with the zinc metal in a similar way.

First we must remember what we mean by a chemical formula. Every element in the Periodic Table can be represented by a short one- or two-letter code, called a **symbol**. The element carbon, for example, is represented by the symbol C.

A **chemical formula** shows the number of each type of atom present in the smallest particle of a substance. For example, the chemical formula for hydrochloric acid is HCl. In the smallest particle of this substance there is one hydrogen atom (whose symbol is H) and one chlorine atom (whose symbol is Cl). But what happens if there is more than one atom of a particular element present?

Let us consider sulfuric acid. The chemical formula for sulfuric acid is H_2SO_4.

A small 2 follows the symbol H for hydrogen – this means there are two hydrogen atoms. The symbol S for sulfur does not have a number after it, so we know there is just one sulfur atom. Finally, a small 4 follows the symbol O for oxygen. This means there are four oxygen atoms.

4 The table below shows the name and formula of a number of different acids. Copy and complete the table, giving the number of each type of atom in the formula of each of the acids.

Name of acid	Formula	Number of each type of atom
hydrochloric acid	HCl	
nitric acid	HNO_3	
sulfuric acid	H_2SO_4	
nitrous acid	HNO_2	
methanoic (formic) acid	CO_2H_2	

What happens when acids react?

The chemical formulas for all the different acids have one thing in common. They all contain hydrogen. In fact, if the metal zinc were placed into any of these acids we would see bubbles of hydrogen gas being released.

In Year 7 you carried out an experiment to test for the colourless, odourless gas hydrogen. When a lighted splint is placed near hydrogen gas it burns with a squeaky pop. This test confirms that the gas is indeed hydrogen. However, the hydrogen gas is not the only new substance made during this chemical reaction. Whenever a metal reacts with an acid, a new compound is also made. After the metal has reacted with the acid and the water has **evaporated**, the tiny crystals of the new compound can be seen.

The new compound belongs to a type of chemicals called **salts**, many of which are soluble.

How are salts named?

The everyday substance we call 'salt' and use to flavour food has the chemical name sodium chloride. This is just one type of salt. It is possible to make many different types of salt. The particular salt made depends on the type of acid and on the type of metal used.

Here are some useful tips for naming salts:

• The first part of the name is the metal used.
• If the acid used was **hydrochloric acid**, the second part of the salt's name is **chloride**.
• If the acid used was **sulfuric acid**, the second part of the salt's name is **sulfate**.
• If the acid used was **nitric acid**, the second part of the salt's name is **nitrate**.

For example, when *zinc* metal reacts with *hydrochloric acid*, the salt **zinc chloride** and the gas hydrogen are formed.

Scientists often use **word equations** to show what happens during chemical reactions. The word equation for this reaction is:

zinc + hydrochloric acid → zinc chloride + hydrogen

The **reactants**, the metal zinc and the hydrochloric acid, are to the left of the arrow. The **products** of the reaction, zinc chloride and hydrogen, are to the right of the arrow.

5 Complete these word equations to show what happens in these reactions.

    a zinc + sulfuric acid → _____ + _____

    b magnesium + hydrochloric acid → _____ + _____

    c calcium + hydrochloric acid → _____ + _____

    d magnesium + nitric acid → _____ + _____

    e magnesium + sulfuric acid → _____ + _____

6 Copy and complete this flow diagram to show the two substances made when a metal reacts with an acid.

    | metal | + | acid | → | ☐ | + | ☐ |

How do metal carbonates react with acids?

When a **metal carbonate** is added to an acid, a chemical reaction takes place.

The bubbles show that a gas is being produced. Can you think of any other ways to tell that a chemical reaction is taking place?

The gas produced is carbon dioxide. We can test for this gas by bubbling it through lime water. When carbon dioxide is bubbled through colourless lime water, the lime water becomes cloudy.

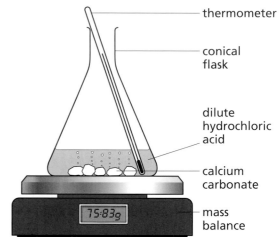

thermometer

conical flask

dilute hydrochloric acid

calcium carbonate

75.83g — mass balance

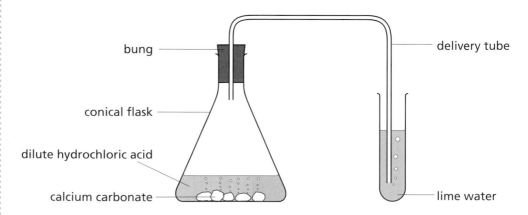

bung

delivery tube

conical flask

dilute hydrochloric acid

calcium carbonate

lime water

In fact, three new substances are made when metal carbonates react with acids – the gas carbon dioxide, some water and a salt.

Predicting the names of salts

Kevin reacted four different metal carbonates with **hydrochloric acid**.

When he added some *magnesium carbonate* to the hydrochloric acid, a chemical reaction took place. The salt magnesium chloride, the gas carbon dioxide and some water were all produced.

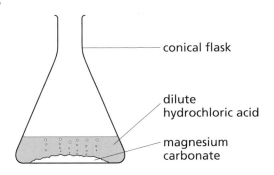

conical flask

dilute hydrochloric acid

magnesium carbonate

Kevin wrote a word equation to show what had happened:

magnesium carbonate + hydrochloric acid → magnesium chloride (a salt) + carbon dioxide + water

Kevin decided to make a different salt. This time he added some *zinc carbonate* to the hydrochloric acid and again a chemical reaction took place. The salt zinc chloride, the gas carbon dioxide and some water were made this time.

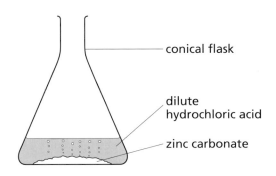

conical flask

dilute hydrochloric acid

zinc carbonate

Here is the word equation for the reaction:

zinc carbonate + hydrochloric acid → zinc chloride (a salt) + carbon dioxide + water

In his next experiment Kevin added some *copper carbonate* to the hydrochloric acid.

The diagram shows Kevin's experiment. We can see that a chemical reaction is taking place because of the bubbles of gas that are being made.

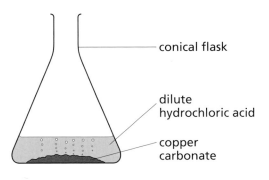

conical flask

dilute hydrochloric acid

copper carbonate

 7 Write a word equation to show what happens in this reaction.

In his final experiment Kevin added some *potassium carbonate* to the hydrochloric acid.

 8 Write a word equation to show what happens in this reaction.

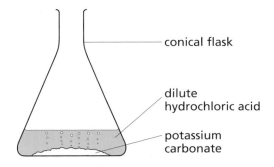

conical flask

dilute hydrochloric acid

potassium carbonate

Sue also carried out some experiments. She always used powdered **calcium carbonate**, but in each experiment she added it to a different acid.

In her first experiment, she added some calcium carbonate to some *hydrochloric acid* and a chemical reaction took place. The salt calcium chloride, the gas carbon dioxide and some water were all made.

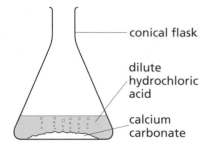

conical flask

dilute hydrochloric acid

calcium carbonate

Sue wrote a word equation to show what had happened:

calcium carbonate + hydrochloric acid → calcium chloride (a salt)
+ carbon dioxide + water

In her second experiment, she added some calcium carbonate to *sulfuric acid*. The salt calcium sulfate, the gas carbon dioxide and some water were all produced by the chemical reaction.

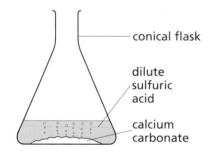

conical flask

dilute sulfuric acid

calcium carbonate

Here is the word equation for this experiment:

calcium carbonate + sulfuric acid → calcium sulfate (a salt)
+ carbon dioxide + water

In her next experiment Sue added some calcium carbonate to some *nitric acid*. In this chemical reaction the salt calcium nitrate, the gas carbon dioxide and some water were all made.

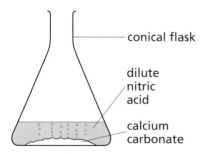

conical flask

dilute nitric acid

calcium carbonate

Sue wrote a word equation to show what had happened:

calcium carbonate + nitric acid → calcium nitrate (a salt)
+ carbon dioxide + water

9 Sue also carried out some reactions using sodium carbonate. She added sodium carbonate to the three different acids. Her experiments are shown in the diagrams below.

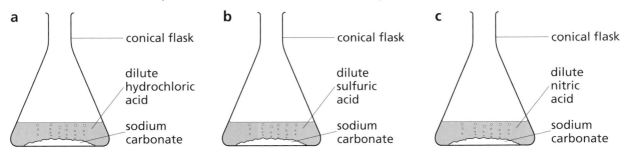

a

conical flask

dilute hydrochloric acid

sodium carbonate

b

conical flask

dilute sulfuric acid

sodium carbonate

c

conical flask

dilute nitric acid

sodium carbonate

Write a word equation to describe what happens in each of these experiments.

10 Copy and complete this flow diagram to show the three substances that are made when a metal carbonate reacts with an acid.

| metal carbonate | + | acid | → | | + | | + | |

How do metal oxides react with acids?

When copper oxide is added to dilute sulfuric acid there is a colour change. This suggests that a chemical reaction has taken place.

When **metal oxides** react with acids, two new substances are made – water and a salt. The salt is soluble, so in order to see it, we must first remove the excess metal oxide that has not reacted with the acid. We can do this by **filtration**. The salt and the water pass through the filter paper, but the insoluble metal oxide collects in the filter paper and can be removed. The salt can be separated from the solution by gently warming the solution. The water **evaporates** and the salt is left behind.

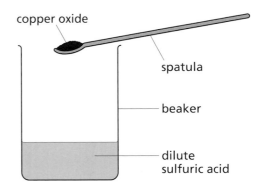

copper oxide

spatula

beaker

dilute sulfuric acid

Crystals of copper sulfate, the salt formed when copper oxide reacts with dilute sulfuric acid.

11 Copy and complete these word equations to show the products made when metal oxides react with acids.

    a magnesium oxide + sulfuric acid → _____ + _____

    b copper oxide + hydrochloric acid → _____ + _____

    c zinc oxide + nitric acid → _____ + _____

    d magnesium oxide + hydrochloric acid → _____ + _____

    e zinc oxide + sulfuric acid → _____ + _____

12 Copy and complete the flow diagram below to show the substances that are made when a metal oxide reacts with an acid.

| metal oxide | + | acid | → | ☐ | + | ☐ |

What is a salt?

When you studied acids and alkalis in Year 7, you learned how to tell whether a solution is acidic or alkaline by adding an indicator to it. One common indicator is called universal indicator.

13 What colour does universal indicator turn in

    a a strongly acidic solution

    b a neutral solution

    c a weakly alkaline solution?

Scientists use a numbered scale, the **pH scale**, to indicate the strength of an acidic or an alkaline solution. On this scale, neutral solutions such as water have a pH of 7. Acidic solutions have a pH value less than 7 and alkaline solutions have a pH value greater than 7.

If the correct amounts of an acid and an alkali are added together, then the alkali 'cancels out' the acid. We say the alkali has **neutralised** the acid.

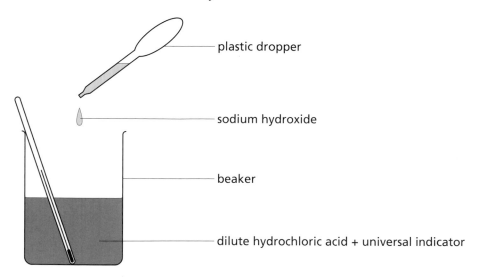

plastic dropper

sodium hydroxide

beaker

dilute hydrochloric acid + universal indicator

When the alkali **sodium hydroxide** is added to dilute hydrochloric acid, the temperature of the solution increases. This tells us that a chemical reaction is taking place, so neutralisation is a chemical reaction. When an alkali and an acid react together, two new substances are made – a salt and water.

The name of the salt can be worked out from the names of the alkali and the acid. In this experiment we have sodium hydroxide and hydrochloric acid. The first part of the salt's name is taken from the metal in the alkali, in this case sodium. The second part of the name comes from the type of acid that is used. As hydrochloric acid is used, this will be a chloride salt. The full name of the salt is sodium chloride.

The word equation for the complete reaction is:

sodium hydroxide + hydro**chlor**ic acid → **sodium chlor**ide + water

If all the alkali reacts with all the acid in this **neutralisation reaction**, then the pH would be 7, or neutral. For this to happen, exactly the right amounts of acid and alkali have to be added together. If an alkali is being added to an acid, then just one drop too much alkali will result in an alkaline solution, and one drop too little alkali still gives an acidic solution. One method of carrying out a neutralisation reaction very accurately is called **titration**.

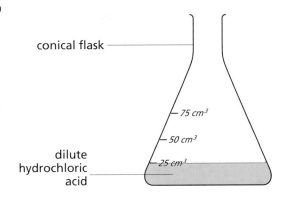

conical flask

75 cm³

50 cm³

dilute hydrochloric acid

25 cm³

First, a measured volume of acid is placed in a flask.

The alkali is poured into a special piece of apparatus called a burette. A burette is a very long glass tube with a tap at the bottom.

This tap can be opened to allow the alkali to slowly drain through. The scale on the burette is used to measure the amount of alkali very accurately.

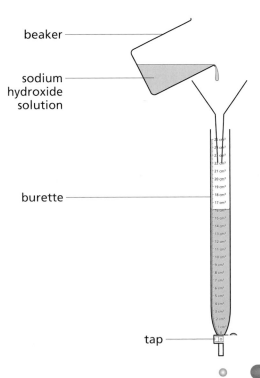

beaker

sodium hydroxide solution

burette

tap

A couple of drops of indicator are added to the acid in the flask, which is placed below the burette. The alkali is then gradually added to the acid. When exactly the right amount of alkali has been added, the indicator changes colour. This shows that a neutral solution of salt and water has been made. The exact amount of alkali used can be worked out from the scale on the burette, so that the reaction can then be repeated quickly. Also, because you know exactly how much alkali is required, there is no need to add an indicator. This means that the salt will be pure, as it does not have an indicator contaminating it.

14 Complete these word equations to show the products made when alkalis react with acids.

a   sodium hydroxide + sulfuric acid → _____ + _____

b   potassium hydroxide + sulfuric acid → _____ + _____

c   potassium hydroxide + hydrochloric acid → _____ + _____

d   calcium hydroxide + sulfuric acid → _____ + _____

e   sodium hydroxide + nitric acid → _____ + _____

15 Copy and complete the flow diagram below to show the substances made when an alkali reacts with an acid.

| alkali | + | acid | → | | + | |

Salts are useful

Scientists can make many different types of salt. Some of these salts are very useful.

- Sodium stearate is used in deodorant sticks.
- Calcium phosphate is made into chinaware.
- Iron sulfate is used in iron tablets to treat people who are anaemic.
- Magnesium sulfate is used to ease constipation.
- Copper sulfate is used in dyeing and in wood preservatives.
- Potassium nitrate is used in gunpowder and fireworks.
- Silver nitrate is used in photography.

How should a salt be made?

Bob has been asked to make two different salts. For each of the salts, he has chosen the chemicals he would use and has written a set of instructions. However, there are some problems with Bob's choice of chemicals and methods.

> To make zinc chloride
> 1 Place some hydrochloric acid in a beaker.
> 2 Add some sodium metal.
> 3 Place the solution you have made into an evaporating basin
> 4 Gently warm the solution until the first crystals appear.
> 5 Leave the solution for a few days for zinc chloride to crystallise.

Sodium metal

Dangerous with water and explosive with acids.

Hydrochloric acid

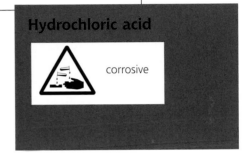

corrosive

> To make copper sulfate
> 1 Place some hydrochloric acid in a beaker.
> 2 Add some copper oxide powder.
> 3 Warm the hydrochloric acid so that the copper oxide dissolves.
> 4 Place the solution you have made into an evaporating basin.
> 5 Fiercely heat the solution until the crystals appear.

Copper oxide

Harmful if swallowed.
Dust irritates lungs and eyes.

Hydrochloric acid

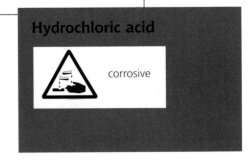

corrosive

YOU MAY BE ABLE TO DO WORKSHEET C10, 'MAKING A SALT'.

16 What are the problems with Bob's plans?

Write a complete set of instructions that should be followed if each salt is to be made safely.

Fireworks!

Firework displays are often used in celebrations such as Guy Fawkes' Night, New Year's Eve and at Diwali.

Creating exciting fireworks involves both science and art. Most fireworks contain several chemicals, including a type of chemical called an oxidiser. Oxidisers are chemicals that release oxygen. Fireworks also include fuels such as sulfur and carbon. These fuels would burn in the air, but they burn even better and reach even higher temperatures when they burn in the oxygen released by the oxidisers.

Perhaps the most stunning aspect of many fireworks is their dazzling range of colours. Metal salts produce these colours; the salts of different metals produce different colours. Copper salts give off blue light, strontium salts give off red light and calcium salts glow orange.

A process called luminescence produces these colours. Inside every atom are tiny particles called electrons. These electrons exist at different energy levels. In the extremely hot conditions inside an exploding firework, some of the electrons in the metal atoms absorb some of the heat energy and move to higher energy levels. Atoms with these electrons are said to have become excited. These excited metal atoms are not very stable, and eventually relax when the electrons fall back to their original energy level. As they do this, the atoms give out the extra energy they had absorbed as a burst of coloured light. The exact amount of energy given out determines the colour of the light. This means that each different metal will give a different colour.

Although fireworks are exciting, they can be dangerous and they cause many terrible accidents every year. Fireworks are explosives and must only be handled carefully – by adults.

a Explain the term 'oxidiser'.
b Name two fuels often used in fireworks.
c What types of salts have been used in the fireworks shown in the photograph?
d Explain the term 'luminescence'.
e Why must fireworks only be used by adults?
f Suggest some safety precautions that adults should take when using fireworks.

Key ideas

Now that you have completed this chapter, you should know:

- which observations show that a chemical reaction is taking place
- which observations to expect when acids react with metals, metal oxides, metal hydroxides and metal carbonates
- how to write general equations to show the reactions between acids and metals, metal oxides, metal hydroxides and metal carbonates
- how to represent, as word equations, the reactions between acids and metals, metal oxides, metal hydroxides and metal carbonates
- how to make predictions about the products of reactions between acids and metals, metal oxides, metal hydroxides and metal carbonates using word equations
- how to test for the gases hydrogen and carbon dioxide
- the names and uses of some different salts
- how to write a plan for preparing a given salt.

Key words

alloy	nitric acid
calcium carbonate	non-metal
chemical formula	pH scale
chemical reaction	potassium hydroxide
copper sulfate	product
evaporate	reactant
filtration	salt
hydrochloric acid	sodium hydroxide
magnesium oxide	sulfuric acid
metal	symbol
metal carbonate	titration
metal oxide	word equation
neutralisation reaction	zinc chloride
neutralise	

1 Rearrange the following anagrams, then write out the word or words and the correct description.

  a tasl   A type of compound formed when an acid reacts with an alkali

  b turpocd   A substance made by a chemical reaction

  c caroneti   A chemical change

  d dosmui echridlo A salt formed when hydrochloric acid is neutralised by sodium hydroxide

  e ygehrodn   The gas produced when a metal reacts with an acid

2 Consider each of these statements. Is it true or false?

  a All salts are actually sodium chloride.

  b All metals are solids at room temperature.

  c When a metal reacts with an acid, a salt and the gas hydrogen are produced.

  d Sulfuric acid makes chloride salts.

  e The test for the gas hydrogen is that it relights a glowing splint.

3 Copy and complete the following sentences.
  When the compound copper oxide is added to dilute hydrochloric acid, a chemical _____ takes place. The acid is gently warmed so that more of the solid dissolves. More copper oxide is added until eventually no more will dissolve. This shows that all the _____ has been used up. The excess copper oxide is then removed by _____. This process produces a solution of the salt, copper chloride and _____. The solution is gently _____ until the first crystals appear. The solution is left near a sunny window for a few days for the copper chloride to _____.

4 These are the steps needed to make the salt copper sulfate from copper carbonate and dilute sulfuric acid, but the order has become confused.
  Put the sentences in the correct order to explain how the salt can be made.

  A It is heated until the first crystals appear.

  B Copper carbonate is added to the dilute sulfuric acid until it stops fizzing.

  C The solution is poured into an evaporating dish.

  D The solution is left for a few days for the copper sulfate to crystallise.

  E The unreacted copper carbonate is removed by filtering.

5 a Which of the following substances are produced when zinc reacts with sulfuric acid?

water   oxygen   zinc oxide   hydrogen   zinc sulfate

b Which of the following substances are produced when zinc carbonate reacts with hydrochloric acid?

carbon dioxide   hydrogen   water   zinc chloride
zinc oxide   copper chloride

6 Copy and complete the following word equations.
a zinc + hydrochloric acid → zinc chloride + _____
b _____ + nitric acid → magnesium nitrate + hydrogen
c calcium carbonate + sulfuric acid → _____ + water
+ carbon dioxide
d zinc carbonate + hydrochloric acid → zinc chloride + _____
+ _____
e copper oxide + _____ → copper sulfate + water

4 Patterns of reactivity

Tutankhamun

Tutankhamun was an Egyptian pharaoh, or king, who lived more than 3300 years ago. He became pharaoh as a child and his reign was brief and largely uneventful. His death, though, is shrouded in mystery. X-rays of the boy's mummified remains have revealed that his skull was fractured. To this day, no one knows for sure whether he was murdered or injured in an accident, such as falling from his horse or chariot.

In 1922 a British explorer, Howard Carter, found the boy king's tomb in the Valley of the Kings. Tutankhamun's mummified remains were discovered in the innermost coffin of three coffins that had been put one inside another. He was wearing this famous mask made from gold, which was found to be completely untarnished even after thousands of years.

The death mask of Tutankhamun.

Why do metals tarnish?

Metals are shiny, strong and good conductors of heat and electricity. These properties mean that metals are used to make many objects.

This silver spoon is about 30 years old.

This bronze statue is more than 60 years old. Bronze is an alloy, or mixture, of two metals – copper and tin.

This gold necklace is over
2000 years old.

This roof is made from the
metal copper. It is over 700 years old.

The gold necklace and Tutankhamun's
gold death mask are still shiny and bright
even after many years, but the
appearance of the other metallic objects
has changed.

This horseshoe is made from
iron. It is just 6 months old.

1 Describe how the appearance of each of the metals has changed over
time. The first one is done for you.

The silver spoon is dull. It has become coated with a dark substance.

If a piece of the
metal sodium is left
in the air, even for a
short time, the
surface of the metal
soon becomes dull.
This photograph
shows how shiny the
freshly cut surface is
compared with the
outer tarnished
surface.

Different metals **react** with air at different rates. Sodium reacts so rapidly
that special steps must be taken to stop any reaction taking place. Sodium
metal is stored in oil to prevent air from coming into contact with it.

2 Look carefully at the photograph and think about the properties
of metals.
   a Explain why sodium is classed as a metallic element.
   b Explain why sodium is an unusual metal.

How do metals react with water?

When a metal such as copper is added to water, nothing happens. There is no chemical reaction between the copper and the water.

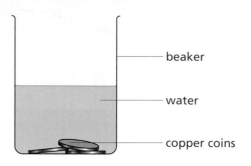

beaker

water

copper coins

However, if an iron nail is left in a beaker of water for a few days, the nail changes colour. This change in colour is evidence of a chemical reaction. The iron is reacting very slowly with the water. The metal zinc also reacts very slowly with water, although it will react more quickly with steam.

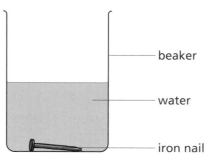

beaker

water

iron nail

However, if a piece of magnesium is placed in water, a chemical reaction takes place and bubbles of a gas can be seen, but you have to look very closely.

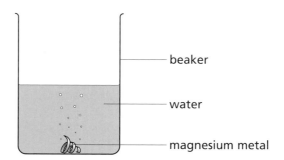

beaker

water

magnesium metal

When lithium is placed in water, a more vigorous reaction takes place and a steady stream of bubbles appears. The beaker containing the reactants also begins to feel a little warmer. The chemical reaction produces two new substances – the gas hydrogen and a solution of lithium hydroxide.

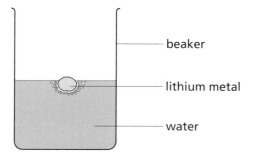

beaker

lithium metal

water

We can test for the hydrogen gas by collecting some in a test tube and holding a lighted splint near it. The hydrogen burns with a squeaky pop. We can test for the lithium hydroxide by adding a few drops of universal indicator. Lithium hydroxide is an alkaline solution and turns the universal indicator purple.

Here is a **word equation** for this reaction:

lithium + water ➜ lithium hydroxide + hydrogen

Sodium also reacts with water. This reaction is very vigorous. The sodium metal whizzes around the surface of the water producing bubbles of hydrogen gas and an alkaline solution of sodium hydroxide.

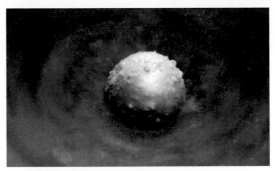

The reaction of sodium with water.

The reaction can be represented by this word equation:

sodium + water → sodium hydroxide + hydrogen

The metal potassium reacts even more violently with water. The potassium often catches fire and burns with a lilac flame. The reaction produces the alkaline solution potassium hydroxide and hydrogen gas.

The reaction of potassium with water.

3 Write a word equation for the reaction of potassium with water.

4 Copy and complete the flow diagram to show the two substances that are made when a metal reacts with water.

| metal | + | water | → | | + | |

5 Describe some of the safety precautions that your science teacher should take when reacting the metal potassium with water.

When metals react with water they produce a metal hydroxide and the gas hydrogen. However, some metals react much more readily than others. The metals that react most vigorously with water are the same metals that tarnish fastest in air. We can use these two sets of reactions to place the metals into an order called the **reactivity series**.

> The *more reactive* a metal is, the *higher its position* in the reactivity series.

6 Place the metals below into a reactivity series, putting the most reactive metal first.

copper   iron   lithium   magnesium   potassium   sodium   zinc

Is the order of reactivity always the same?

You have already studied the reactions between acids and metals.

When a metal such as zinc is placed in dilute hydrochloric acid, bubbles can be seen. These bubbles show that a chemical reaction is taking place. Hydrogen gas and the salt zinc chloride are produced.

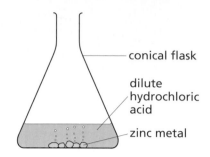
conical flask

dilute hydrochloric acid

zinc metal

7 Write a word equation for this reaction.

We have seen that metals can be placed into an **order of reactivity**. For the metals copper, iron, magnesium and zinc reacting with air and with water, the order is:

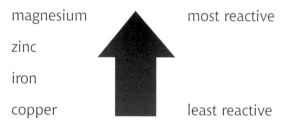

magnesium   most reactive

zinc

iron

copper   least reactive

Is the order of reactivity the same when these metals react with acid?

This diagram shows what happens when these four metals are placed in test tubes of hydrochloric acid.

dilute hydrochloric acid

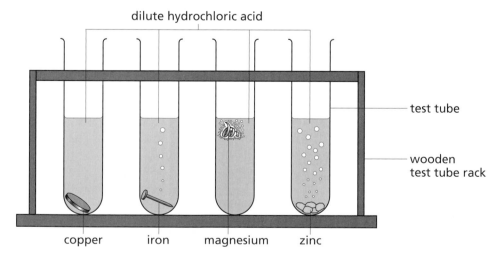

test tube

wooden test tube rack

copper   iron   magnesium   zinc

8 a Which of these metals react with hydrochloric acid?
  b Explain how you can tell which of the metals react.
  c Write a word equation for the reaction between the metal magnesium and hydrochloric acid.
  d Place these four metals into an order of reactivity based on their reactions with hydrochloric acid. Put the most reactive metal first.
  e Compare your order of reactivity for the metals with acid with the order of reactivity of the metals with air and with water.

How do metals react with oxygen?

When metals burn, they react with the oxygen in the air. A new substance called an **oxide** is formed. You may remember burning the silvery metal called magnesium. Magnesium burns in air with a brilliant white flame. It is quite an exciting and vigorous reaction. The new substance made by the reaction is a white powder called magnesium oxide.

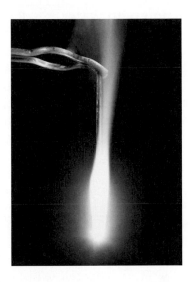

 9 Write a word equation for this reaction.

We have seen that metals can be placed into an order of reactivity based on their reactions with air, water and acid. We can use this order to **predict** how these metals will react when they are burnt. The metal copper did not react with water or with acid, so it was placed below magnesium and at the bottom of the reactivity series. From this, we could predict that copper would probably react more slowly than magnesium when it is burnt.

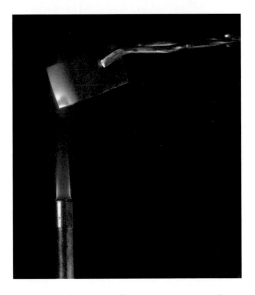

When the metal copper is placed in a Bunsen burner flame, not much happens. After a while, the copper begins to glow red and eventually it turns black. This reaction is much less vigorous than the reaction between magnesium and oxygen.

 10 a What is the black substance called?
b Write a word equation for this reaction.

11 a The metal sodium is higher in the reactivity series than magnesium. How would you expect sodium to react if it was burnt?
b Would it be sensible to carry out this reaction yourself?

From these reactions we can see that being able to put metals in an order of reactivity can be very useful for predicting other reactions.

12 This table shows some of the reactions of four metals.

Metal	Reaction with water	Reaction with acid	Reaction when heated in air
A	No reaction	Very slow reaction. A few bubbles of gas are given off.	Burns and produces a metal oxide.
B	Very slow reaction. A few bubbles of gas are given off.	Vigorous reaction. Many bubbles of gas are given off.	Vigorous reaction. Burns with a brilliant white flame and produces a metal oxide.
C	No reaction	No reaction	Slow reaction. Glows red and produces a metal oxide.
D	No reaction	No reaction	No reaction

a Use the information in the table to place the metals in order of reactivity. Put the most reactive metal first.
b Metal E is to be included in the list. The metal reacts vigorously with water and violently with acid. Rewrite your original order of reactivity to include metal E.
c Predict how the metal E will react when it is burnt in air.

Competition between metals

When an iron nail is added to a solution of **copper sulfate**, a chemical reaction takes place, and both the nail and the solution change colour.

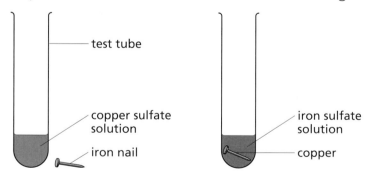

test tube

copper sulfate solution

iron nail

iron sulfate solution

copper

The iron nail is covered with a brown substance. This brown substance is a metal. It is not rust – it is copper. The solution is now a pale green colour. The solution is **iron sulfate**.

Here is the word equation for the reaction:

iron + copper sulfate → iron sulfate + copper

This is an example of a **displacement reaction**. Iron is a more reactive metal than copper. When the iron nail is placed into the copper sulfate solution, the more reactive metal, iron, displaces the less reactive metal, copper, from the copper sulfate.

YOU MAY BE ABLE TO DO WORKSHEET D7, 'DISPLACEMENT REACTIONS'.

But, if a copper coin is placed in an iron sulfate solution, nothing happens. The copper is less reactive than the iron, so copper cannot displace iron from the iron sulfate, and there is no reaction.

> A more reactive metal *competes* with a less reactive metal and will *displace* it from its compounds.

We can use this idea to predict whether or not a reaction will occur.

13 a Tom has four different metals and four different metal sulfate solutions. He places a couple of drops of each solution onto a spotting tile and then adds a small piece of each metal. He has designed this table to record his results.
Copy and complete the table by adding a tick if you predict that there will be a reaction and a cross if you predict there will be no reaction. The reaction between iron and copper sulfate has been completed for you.

Metal sulfate solution / Metal	copper sulfate	magnesium sulfate	iron sulfate	zinc sulfate
copper				
magnesium				
iron	✔			
zinc				

b Write word equations for all of the reactions that you have predicted will occur.

Using displacement reactions

Some displacement reactions can be very useful. One such example is the **thermit reaction**, which is used to repair iron railway tracks. In this reaction, aluminium is heated with **iron oxide**. The aluminium is more reactive than the iron, and displaces the iron from the iron oxide. Aluminium oxide and iron are produced.

Thermit reaction being used to mend railway tracks.

Here is the word equation for this reaction:

aluminium + iron oxide → aluminium oxide + iron

This reaction gives out so much heat that the iron made is actually molten. This means that the iron can be poured straight into the gaps in the railway tracks where it is needed.

How does the reactivity of a metal relate to its use?

There are more than eighty different metals, and many of them play an enormously important role in our lives.

The way we use a particular metal depends on its properties and on how reactive that metal is.

14 These diagrams show the uses of some different metals. Look carefully at the diagrams and at the descriptions of the different metals in the table.
Copy and complete the table by matching the metal to its use.

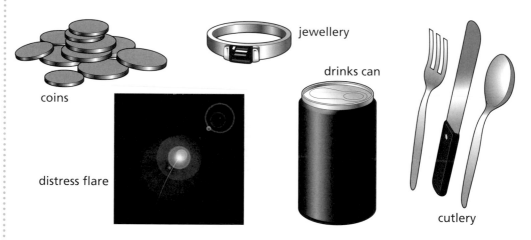

coins

jewellery

drinks can

distress flare

cutlery

Metal	Description	Use
magnesium	Reacts vigorously when it is burnt in air.	
steel	It is strong and does not react readily with water or with air.	
copper	Unreactive and hard wearing and does not react with air, water or acids.	
platinum	Very unreactive and does not tarnish in air. Can easily be shaped.	
aluminium	Reacts quickly with air to form an oxide layer, which prevents any further reactions. Lightweight.	

15 Find out about the uses of some different metals. Produce a leaflet showing how the reactivity of different metals relates to their uses.

Why do some metals appear to be less reactive than expected?

We can use the reactivity series to predict how metals will react.

Here is a part of the reactivity series showing the reactivity of three metals.

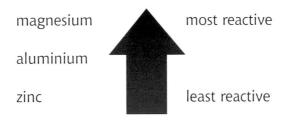

magnesium   most reactive

aluminium

zinc   least reactive

When metals react with acid, a chemical reaction takes place. This reaction produces bubbles of hydrogen gas and a salt. We can measure how vigorously each metal reacts with acid by counting the number of gas bubbles produced each minute when each metal is placed in acid.

16 How would you make sure that this was a fair test?

17 Use the reactivity series to predict how each metal will react.

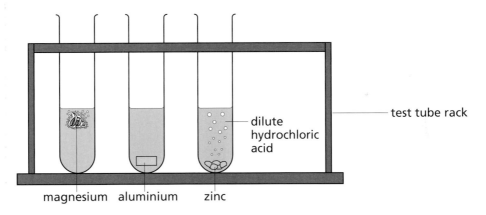

test tube rack

dilute hydrochloric acid

magnesium   aluminium   zinc

When the metals are added to the acid, the results are a little surprising. Magnesium reacts vigorously with the acid, producing many bubbles of hydrogen gas. However, the second most reactive metal appears to be zinc. The zinc reacts with the acid producing a steady stream of bubbles. The aluminium does not appear to react at all.

18 Compare these results with your predictions.

In fact, aluminium often appears to be less reactive than it really is. This is because aluminium quickly reacts with the oxygen in the air to produce a protective layer of aluminium oxide. This layer coats the surface and so prevents any further reaction when the metal is placed in the acid. This is why it is quite safe to keep acidic fizzy drinks in aluminium cans.

The discovery of metals

The oldest metals known to man are gold and copper. Gold is such an unreactive metal that it can be found pure and uncombined with any other elements. There is evidence that Stone Age people found gold nuggets in river beds more than 6000 years ago. Pure gold is quite soft, so they could shape it easily. Because gold is so unreactive, it did not tarnish but retained its bright shiny colour. It was very rare and so was highly prized. It is too soft to be suitable for making tools, but was used to make jewellery, just as it is today – though now it is used as an alloy to make it harder.

Copper is also very unreactive. Some can be found uncombined, but most copper is found in minerals, such as malachite. Pure copper can be extracted from malachite by heating the mineral in a fire. Copper was more useful than gold as it could be used to make tools and weapons because it is harder.

The later discovery of tin heralded the Bronze Age. Bronze is an alloy of the two elements copper and tin. It was discovered when rocks containing both copper minerals and tin minerals were heated together. Bronze is much harder and stronger than pure copper. By 1400 BC it was the most widely used metal alloy in the world.

The next great breakthrough was the discovery of iron. A little impure iron had been found in meteorites but iron could not be extracted in large amounts until people started to use coal fires. Coal burns at a much higher temperature than wood or charcoal. Iron was used to make weapons and tools, which revolutionised the world in the Iron Age.

Gradually, over the next three thousand years, other metals were discovered. The next major advance occurred at the beginning of the eighteenth century. Until electricity was discovered, no one had been able to isolate any of the reactive metals used so widely today. Metals like aluminium are so reactive that they are never found free in nature. They cannot be extracted by simply heating their minerals and are too reactive to be extracted by heating their ores with coal. They can only be extracted by splitting their minerals or ores using electricity in a process called **electrolysis**.

In general, the more reactive a metal is, the harder it is to extract from its ore and the more recently it has been discovered.

a How was the metal gold found and used by Stone Age people?
b What is bronze and why was its discovery important?
c How can iron be extracted and why was it only discovered after tin?
d Sodium was discovered in 1807 by Sir Humphry Davy. Suggest how sodium should be extracted from its ore.
e Explain the connection between the reactivity of a metal and its date of discovery.
f Find out about some of the other discoveries of Sir Humphry Davy.

Key ideas

Now that you have completed this chapter, you should know how to:

- describe the reactions of metals with water, acids and oxygen

- represent these reactions using word equations

- describe the similarities and differences between the reactions of different metals that allow them to be placed into an order of reactivity

- relate the reactivity of a metal to its use

- explain how the reactivity of a metal affects the state in which it is found in nature and how it must be extracted, and how a metal's reactivity relates to the date of its discovery

- use the reactivity series to make predictions about how metals will react.

Key words

copper sulfate	oxide
displacement reaction	predict
electrolysis	react
iron oxide	reactivity series
iron sulfate	thermit reaction
magnesium sulfate	word equation
order of reactivity	zinc sulfate

1 Rearrange the following anagrams then write out the word or words and the correct description.

itarcityev iesers   diorepcitn   titemrh arcnotei   elidaescpmnt lytilseceros

a A way of splitting up a substance using electricity.

b A list in which metals are placed in order from most to least reactive.

c A type of reaction in which a more reactive metal takes the place of a less reactive metal.

d A useful displacement reaction in which aluminium displaces iron from iron oxide.

e What you expect to happen.

2 Consider each of these statements. Is it true or false?

a When an iron nail is placed into copper sulfate solution, the brown substance formed on the nail is rust.

b The metal potassium is suitable for making boats.

c Bronze was discovered after gold.

d When a metal reacts with water, the gas produced is hydrogen.

e Iron will tarnish faster than gold.

3 The names of six metals have been hidden in this wordsearch. Find the names and then place them in order of reactivity. Place the most reactive metal first.

n	m	o	e	c	v
m	u	i	d	o	s
k	i	f	t	p	v
m	s	b	c	p	h
c	e	d	w	e	x
n	n	s	l	r	n
i	g	i	l	o	h
z	a	u	r	u	g
d	m	i	f	y	m

4 The diagram below shows the order of reactivity of five metals.

magnesium   most reactive
aluminium
zinc
iron
copper   least reactive

Copy and complete these word equations using the information in the diagram above.

a magnesium + iron sulfate →
b aluminium + iron oxide →
c zinc + copper sulfate →
d magnesium + zinc sulfate →
e zinc + iron sulfate →

5 Read the following passage carefully and then place the metals A, B, C and D in order of reactivity. Place the most reactive metal first.

Metal A displaced metal C from a solution of its sulfate.
Metal B reacts faster with hydrochloric acid than metal A.
Metal D does *not* react when it is heated with the oxide of metal C.

6 Use pictures from catalogues and magazines to make a poster to show the uses of some different metals. Place the metals in order of their reactivity.

5 Pressure and moments

This manned submersible research vessel is capable of working at more than 1000 m below the surface of the sea. It is used to investigate the depths of the world's oceans. It has been designed to withstand enormous pressures from the water around it. In the first part of this chapter we shall discover how forces create pressures.

When we apply a force to an object, the effect of that force often depends on the area over which it is applied. **Pressure** is a measure of 'how concentrated' a force is. If a force is concentrated over a *small* area it will create a *high* pressure, but if the same force is spread over a *larger* area it will create a *lower* pressure.

The weight of the man on the left is spread over a large area because he is wearing snowshoes. The pressure beneath his snowshoes is quite small, so he does not sink into the snow. The weight of the man on the right is concentrated over a smaller area. The pressure beneath his shoes is much greater and he has sunk into the snow.

When this boy walked out onto the ice, his weight was concentrated over a small area (the soles of his shoes) and so created a high pressure. This pressure was high enough to crack the ice! His rescuer is crawling along a ladder to reach him. The ladder spreads the man's weight over a very large area and so creates a much smaller pressure.

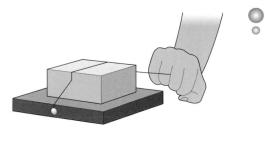

You may be able to do Worksheet E1, 'Creating pressures'.

The force applied through this wire to the cheese is concentrated over a very small area and so creates the large pressure needed to cut through the cheese.

The narrow handles of some bags can create painfully high pressures across the palms of your hands and across your fingers. If the handles were wider, the weight would be spread over a larger area and so the pressure would be reduced.

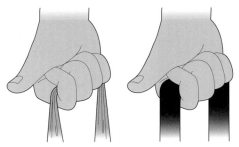

The sharp spikes or crampons worn by this climber concentrate his weight over a very small area, creating very high pressures. These pressures cause the points or spikes to dig into the hard surface of the ice so that he does not slip.

1 a Give two examples of situations where it is an advantage to have high pressures.

b Give two examples of situations where it is a disadvantage to have high pressures.

c This diagram shows an Indian fakir lying on a bed of nails.

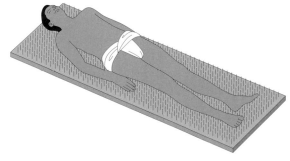

Explain why the points of the nails do not puncture his skin.

Calculating pressures

To calculate the pressure created by a force we use the equation:

$$\textbf{Pressure} = \frac{\textbf{force}}{\textbf{area}}$$

This equation can be usefully written as a formula triangle:

From this we can see that $F = P \times A$ and $A = \dfrac{F}{P}$

The force is measured in newtons, the area in metres squared and the pressure is measured in **pascals** (**Pa**) where 1 Pa is one **newton** per metre squared.

Example
Calculate the pressure created when a force of 20 N is applied to an area of 4m².

$$\text{Pressure} = \frac{\text{force}}{\text{area}}$$

$$= \frac{20\,\text{N}}{4\,\text{m}^2} = 5\,\text{Pa}$$

2 Calculate the pressures created by these forces.

a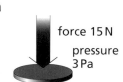
force 10 N
area 5 m²

b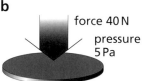
force 18 N
area 6 m²

c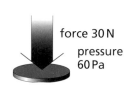
force 24 N
area 10 m²

3 Calculate the area over which each of these forces is being applied in order to produce the pressure indicated.

a
force 15 N
pressure 3 Pa

b
force 40 N
pressure 5 Pa

c
force 30 N
pressure 60 Pa

4 Calculate the size of each applied force.

a
area 4 m²
pressure 4 Pa

b
area 2.5 m²
pressure 8 Pa

c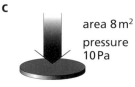
area 8 m²
pressure 10 Pa

You may be able to do Worksheet E2, 'The formula triangle for pressure'.

Pressure in liquids

When an object is immersed in a liquid, the liquid exerts a pressure on it. This pressure is caused by the liquid particles colliding with the object. The size of the pressure these particles exert on the object depends upon the density of the liquid and how far below the surface they are.

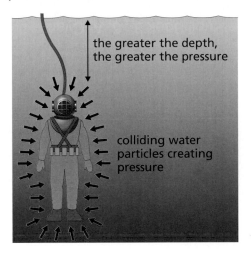

the greater the depth, the greater the pressure

colliding water particles creating pressure

Liquid rushes out of the holes at the bottom of this can faster than from those at the top. This shows that the pressure in a liquid increases with depth.

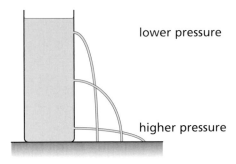

lower pressure

higher pressure

The liquid in this can rushes out of both the holes at the same speed. The holes are at the same depth but they are in different directions. This shows that the pressure in a liquid is the same in all directions.

5 Which part of a dam wall is thickest? Give a reason for your answer. Use a diagram to show the cross-section of the dam wall.

6 A diver takes a large spherical balloon down to the ocean bed. Explain how
   a the size
   b the shape
   of the balloon changes as it is taken deeper under the water.

The particles in a liquid are quite close together. So, if a force is applied to a liquid, it is almost impossible to squash it. We say that liquids are **incompressible**. This property of a liquid can be very useful. The study of pressures in liquids is called **hydraulics**.

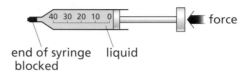

Even when a large force is applied to the piston, it will not move because the liquid is incompressible.

These examples show how useful liquids are in exerting pressures and forces.

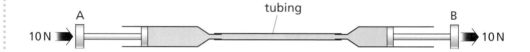

If a force of 10 N is applied at A, a force of 10 N is exerted at B.

This is also true if the pipe is not straight, so liquids can be used to change the direction of a force.

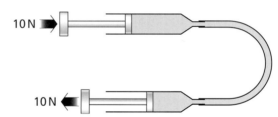

If the pipe divides into several branches which are all of the same cross-sectional area, the applied force of 10 N is now exerted at the ends of all the other pipes, that is at X, Y, and Z.

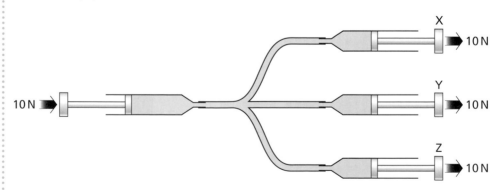

If the cross-sectional area of the piston is changed, so too is the size of the force exerted.

In this diagram, a force of 10 N is applied at C, causing a force of 20 N to be exerted at D. An arrangement of pipes and liquid like this can be used to increase the size of an applied force.

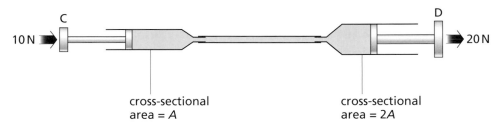

A machine used in this way is called a **force multiplier**. A good example of this is the **hydraulic jack**. Because they increase the size of the applied force, hydraulic jacks are used to lift cars.

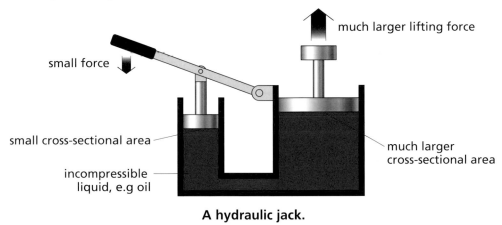

A hydraulic jack.

Most modern cars have hydraulic brakes. The advantages of using these are:

• A small force applied to the brake pedal can be increased to create a large braking force, so the driver does not need to be very strong to make a car stop quickly.
• The force applied to each wheel can be adjusted to be the same.

7 Why are liquids incompressible?
8 Give two advantages of transmitting pressures and forces through liquids.

Pneumatics

The particles in gases are far apart. So, if a force is applied to a gas, it will be squashed. We say that gases are **compressible**.

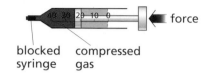

blocked syringe   compressed gas   force

The study of pressures in gases is called **pneumatics**.

The pressure of gases, like liquids, is caused by the collisions of its particles. The air around us is continually applying a pressure, but we are so used to it that we are almost unaware of its presence. We call this pressure **atmospheric pressure**.

This simple experiment demonstrates that atmospheric pressure exists.

Air molecules are continually colliding with both the inside and the outside walls of the empty plastic bottle. Because the pressures are the same, the bottle keeps its shape. If the air particles inside the bottle are removed, the pressure from the air particles outside the bottle causes the sides of the bottle to buckle inwards.

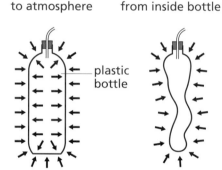

tubing open to atmosphere   air particles removed from inside bottle

plastic bottle

In 1657 Otto von Guericke carried out an experiment to demonstrate how large atmospheric pressure is. He made a sphere in two halves, with a tap in one of the halves. When the two halves were placed together they made an airtight seal. Air was then pumped out of the sphere through the tap. Air pressure on the outside of the sphere now held the two halves together very tightly. So strong is atmospheric pressure that two teams of eight horses were unable to separate the hemispheres. But, when the tap was opened and air rushed into the sphere, the two halves were pulled apart with almost no effort.

We make use of the pressure of a gas and atmospheric pressure in many everyday situations. Some are shown in the diagrams below.

9 Why are gases compressible?

10 What is atmospheric pressure?

Moments

Look carefully at all these diagrams. What do they have in common?

In each situation the applied force is creating a turning motion. This turning effect of a force is called a **moment**.

The size of a moment depends upon:

- the size of the applied force
- the perpendicular distance of the applied force from the **pivot**.

The pivot is the point around which an object is turning.

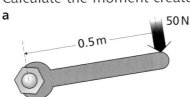

We calculate the size of the moment created by a force using the equation:

Moment = force × perpendicular distance from pivot

Moment = $F \times d$

Example

A force of 50 N is applied to these spanners.

Calculate the moment created by the force in each case.

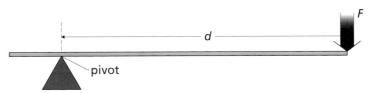
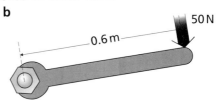

a Moment = $F \times d$

 = 50 N × 0.5 m

 = 25 N m

b Moment = $F \times d$

 = 50 N × 0.6 m

 = 30 N m

You MAY BE ABLE TO DO WORKSHEETS E3, 'THE TURNING EFFECT OF A FORCE'.

We can see why it is an advantage to use a long spanner to undo a stiff nut – the same force creates a larger moment with the longer spanner.

11 Calculate the moment created in each of these situations.

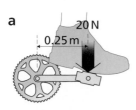

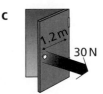

Levers

Levers are simple machines. They are pieces of equipment that help us to do something more easily.

This man is trying to open a tin of paint. Unaided it is almost impossible, but by using a screwdriver as a simple lever, the task is much easier.

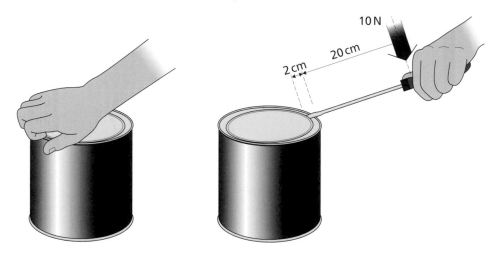

The moment created by the applied force is 10 N x 20 cm = 200 N cm. This moment creates a force F that is applied upwards to the tin lid.

So 200 N cm $= F \times 2$ cm

$$F = \frac{200 \, \text{N cm}}{2 \, \text{cm}}$$

$$= 100 \, \text{N}$$

A downward force of 10 N applied to one end of the screwdriver creates an upward force of 100 N at the other end of the screwdriver. The lever is acting as a **force multiplier**.

12 Calculate the upward force, F, created by the lever in each of these situations.

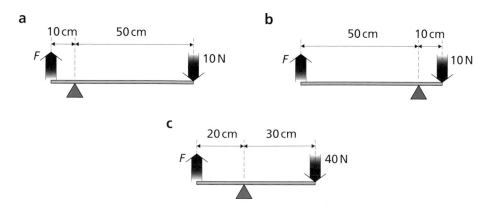

You may be able to do Worksheet E4, 'Levers'.

Levers in the body

Muscles in our bodies often create turning effects.

When this athlete lifts the weight, his biceps muscles contract and his triceps relax, creating a moment about his elbow – his arm is acting as a lever.

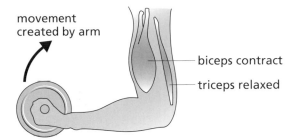

movement created by arm

biceps contract

triceps relaxed

Pairs of muscles like the biceps and triceps are called **antagonistic muscles** as they work in opposite directions to produce movement.

Balance

How is this man able to walk on a rope? It is all a question of **balance** – but how do you keep your balance?

To explain how the man is able to walk along a rope we must first understand the phrase '**centre of gravity**'. This is a point within an object where we imagine all its weight to be concentrated.

For regular shapes such as spheres and cubes, the centre of gravity is at the geometric centre of the object.

Tightrope walker in Mexico City.

YOU MAY BE ABLE TO DO WORKSHEET E5, 'FINDING THE CENTRE OF GRAVITY OF AN OBJECT'.

For non-uniform shapes, the position of the centre of gravity depends on the shape of the object and how the weight of the object is distributed. The centre of gravity for most people is approximately level with their tummy button.

The tightrope walker must keep his centre of gravity directly above the rope, so there is no moment causing him to topple. If his centre of gravity moves so that it is not directly above the rope, it creates a moment and he will lose his balance.

13 What are antagonistic muscles?
14 What is the centre of gravity of an object? Where is the centre of gravity of a sphere?
15 Why does a tightrope walker carry a pole? What does he do with it?

If we tilt an object through a small angle and it falls over when we release it, we say that the object is **unstable**. If we can tilt an object through a fairly large angle and it falls back to its original position when we release it, we can say that the object is **stable**.

If we let go of this bottle it will topple over as its weight is creating a 'toppling' moment around P.

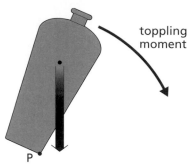

toppling moment

If we let go of this bottle it will not topple over as its weight is creating a 'restoring' moment around P.

restoring moment

For an object to be stable:

• its centre of gravity should be as low as possible
• it should have a wide base.

These features are clearly demonstrated in the way that racing cars have been developed. The earlier cars were box-shaped with a high centre of gravity. These cars were liable to tip over if they turned a corner too fast. Modern racing cars are much more stable than earlier cars as they have a much wider wheel base and their centre of gravity is much closer to the ground.

Bugatti Brescia racing car from 1923.

Formula 1 racing car from 2003.

16 Draw a diagram of two objects – one which is unstable and one which is stable.

17 Explain why the centre of gravity of a double-decker bus is quite low.

Balancing moments

The two pupils on the see-saw are both creating moments about P. The boy is creating a clockwise moment and the girl an anticlockwise moment. If these two moments are equal, the see-saw will balance.

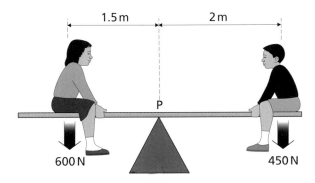

Clockwise moment $= 450 \times 2 = 900\,\text{N m}$

Anticlockwise moment $= 600 \times 1.5 = 900\,\text{N m}$

The two moments are equal, so the see-saw balances.

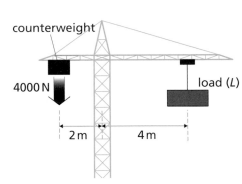

When the crane in the diagram lifts the load, *L*, a clockwise moment is created. To prevent the crane from toppling it has a **counterweight**. The counterweight can be moved to create an equal and opposite moment to that created by the load.

YOU MAY BE ABLE TO DO WORKSHEET E6, 'BALANCING MOMENTS'.

Example
Calculate the maximum load, *L*, this crane can lift with the counterweight in its present position.

At balance, the anticlockwise moments = the clockwise moments

$$4000 \times 2 = L \times 4$$

$$\text{So } L = 2000\,\text{N}$$

18 If the girl on the see-saw above moves so that she is 1 m from the pivot P, where must the boy sit in order to balance the see-saw?

The bends

A diver at sea level experiences a pressure of 1 atmosphere due to the air particles around him. Below the surface of the sea, he experiences greater pressures due to the water particles – the deeper he dives, the greater these pressures become. At a depth of approximately 10 m, the total pressure is 2 atmospheres, whilst at a depth of 20 m it is 3 atmospheres.

If the diver is using SCUBA gear (self-contained underwater breathing apparatus) the air from the tanks he uses automatically comes out at the same pressure as the water around it. Under these circumstances more gas particles than normal dissolve in the bloodstream and body tissue.

At depths greater than 30 m these extra particles can cause problems. If a diver who has been at a depth of more than 30 m for some time returns to the surface rapidly, the excess dissolved gas is released in the same way that the gas from a fizzy drink is released when you shake the bottle or can and then open it. In the diver, this sudden decompression and the gas bubbles formed in the tissues of the nervous system can cause a very painful and dangerous condition called the bends.

To avoid this problem, divers must rise slowly or make several stops on their way to the surface to allow the excess gas to escape slowly. If a diver has to surface quickly, he must enter a decompression chamber in which the air is at the same pressure he experienced during his dive. This pressure is then gradually released.

Inside a decompression chamber.

a What is the origin of the word scuba?
b At what pressure is the air in the tanks of a scuba diver released?
c What is the approximate pressure exerted on a diver 30 m below the surface of the sea?
d What causes a diver to suffer from the bends?
e How can a diver avoid the bends?
f Explain why it is a good idea for divers not to travel by air immediately after completing a deep dive.

Key ideas

Now that you have completed this chapter, you should know:

- how the effect of a force depends on the area over which it is applied
- the relationship between pressure, force and area
- examples of situations where high or low pressures are desirable and how they are achieved
- that liquids are incompressible, but gases can be compressed
- that pressures can be transmitted by liquids, and describe examples such as the hydraulic jack, hydraulic brakes
- that gases exert pressures, and can explain how they do this using the particle theory
- about atmospheric pressure and some of its effects
- that the turning effect of a force is called a moment, and be able to give everyday examples of where moments are created
- the relationship between the size of a force, its perpendicular distance from the pivot and the moment it creates
- how a lever works and be able to give several examples of everyday levers
- the factors that affect the stability or balance of an object
- that an object such as a see-saw is balanced when the moments trying to turn it clockwise are equal to moments trying to turn it anticlockwise.

Key words

antagonistic muscles	incompressible
atmospheric pressure	lever
balance	moment
balancing moments	newton (N)
centre of gravity	pascal (Pa)
compressible	pivot
counterweight	pneumatics
force multiplier	pressure
hydraulic jack	stable
hydraulics	unstable

1 This young man is in a lot of pain, but which foot is hurting more?

2 Why is kneeling for a long time on a hard floor much more uncomfortable than lying on the same floor?

3 Explain why swimmers sometimes complain of discomfort in their ears when they dive to the bottom at the deep end of a swimming pool.

4 What is the role of pressure in:
   a a sharp knife
   b a drawing pin
   c a camel's feet?

5 Explain why it is a bad idea to throw a pressurised container such as an aerosol can onto a fire.

6 Calculate the force that must be applied to this hydraulic jack in order to lift the 800 N weight.

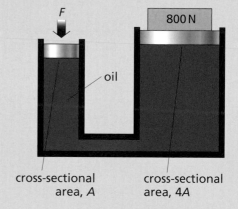

cross-sectional area, A cross-sectional area, $4A$

7 Make a list of five objects in your house that act as levers.

8 If you place your finger under the 50 cm mark on a metre rule, the rule will balance. Explain why.

9 Why is this athlete in danger of falling from the beam? Explain what she can do in order to avoid losing her balance.

centre of gravity

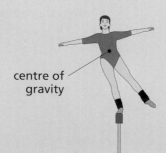

6 Inheritance and selection

All the people in this photograph are related to each other. They are all members of the same family.

1 a Describe one physical feature shared by some of these family members that might give you a clue that they are related to each other.
  b Why do you think they all share this feature?
  c How do the members of the family differ from each other?
  d Suggest what might cause these differences between them.

You already know that we refer to the differences between members of the same species – including humans – as **variation**. Variation can be caused by two different factors. These two factors are **genes** and the **environment**.

Because the people in the photograph are all related to each other, they all share some of the same genes for physical features – the genes that affect the way that we look.

Genes and reproduction

What are genes?

All the cells in your body have the same set of genes. Genes are inside the nucleus of each cell.

Genes are made of a chemical called **DNA**. Long strands of DNA form the **chromosomes** inside the nuclei of your cells. Humans have 46 chromosomes inside the nucleus of each cell. Each chromosome contains hundreds of genes.

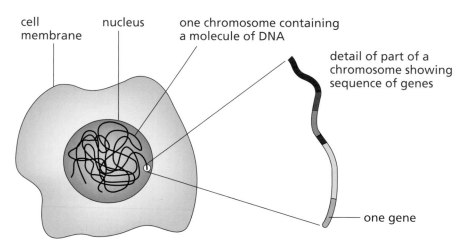

cell membrane

nucleus

one chromosome containing a molecule of DNA

detail of part of a chromosome showing sequence of genes

one gene

Each gene is a set of instructions telling the cell to do something. Some of these instructions have an effect on your appearance. For example, some of your genes tell the cells in your skin what colour hair to make. Some of your genes tell your nose what shape to grow into.

Where do your genes come from?

You inherited your genes from your parents. You began when a sperm cell from your father fused with an egg cell from your mother. The sperm cell's nucleus contained a set of genes from your father, while the egg cell's nucleus contained a set of genes from your mother.

> Sperm cells and egg cells are sex cells. Another name for them is **gametes**. A sperm cell is a male gamete, while an egg cell is a female gamete.

When the nuclei of the sperm cell and the egg cell fused together, they made a new cell called a **zygote**. The nucleus of the zygote contained the two sets of genes – one set each from your mother and father.

The zygote divided over and over again to form all the cells in your body. Each time it divided, all the genes were copied exactly, so that each new cell contained exactly the same genes as the zygote. Now your body contains millions of cells, each containing a set of genes from your father and a set of genes from your mother.

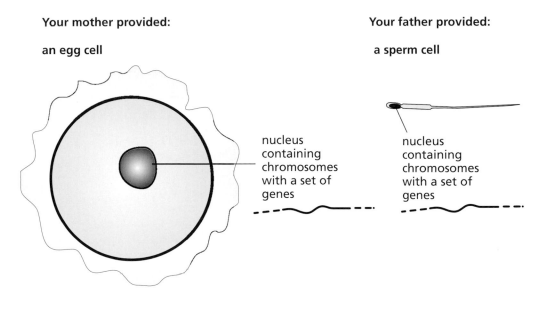

Your mother provided:

an egg cell

Your father provided:

a sperm cell

nucleus containing chromosomes with a set of genes

nucleus containing chromosomes with a set of genes

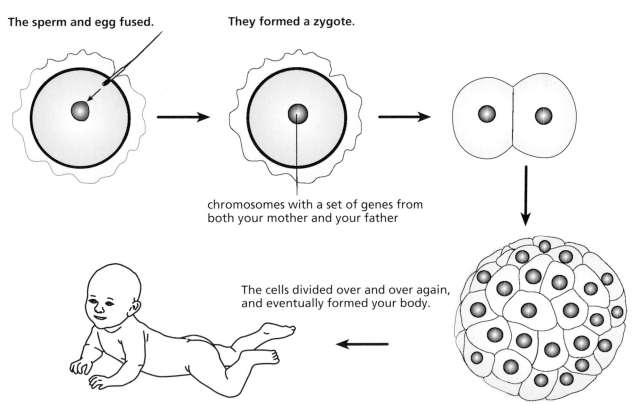

The sperm and egg fused.

They formed a zygote.

chromosomes with a set of genes from both your mother and your father

The cells divided over and over again, and eventually formed your body.

So every cell in your body contains a set of genes from your mother, and a set of genes from your father.

Twins

These diagrams show two different ways in which twins can be formed.

How non-identical twins are produced

Both ovaries release an egg cell at the same time and both are fertilised.

How identical twins are produced

One egg is fertilised but the first two cells separate, then continue to develop separately.

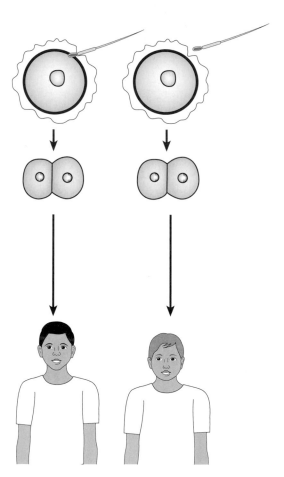
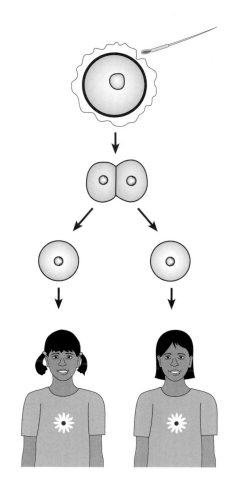

2 a Why are identical twins identical?
  b What determines what sex you are – your genes or your environment?
  c Could identical twins be different sexes?

Breeding new varieties

Humans use many different kinds of plants and animals. Here are some examples.

Wheat is grown to produce seeds (grains) for making flour. The grains of this variety of wheat have an especially high amount of a protein called gluten, which helps to make excellent bread.

Horses are kept for pleasure. This horse is a thoroughbred, and has been bred to run fast and win races.

Cattle are kept to give milk and meat for food. This variety of cattle is called Holstein. The cows give large amounts of high-quality milk.

Sheep are kept to give wool and meat. This variety of sheep is called Swaledale. They are particularly suited to hilly areas because they can survive on quite poor-quality grass and in cold temperatures.

YOU MAY BE ABLE TO DO WORKSHEET F4, 'COMPARING FRUIT OR VEGETABLE VARIETIES'.

Where did all these different varieties come from?

Apples are grown to eat. This variety is called Cox. They are popular because they have a very good flavour.

Domesticating animals and plants

Until about 10 000 years ago, humans simply collected the food they could find in their environment. They gathered berries, fruits and roots. They killed animals for food.

Then people began to take more control over their food. They learnt to collect seeds of the plants that they liked eating, and sowed them near where they lived. This meant that they did not have to go so far to find the plants, and that a large number of the same plant could be grown in a small area. They could help the plants to grow well by removing weeds, so the plants they wanted did not have to compete for light, water or nutrients with the plants they did not want.

Early humans did a similar thing with animals. Sheep and cattle live naturally in herds, so it was not difficult to keep groups of them together in one place. These early farmers could make sure that their animals had water and food.

Selective breeding

All this was happening long before anyone knew about chromosomes, genes or zygotes. However, people *did* notice that their plants and animals varied. For example, they might see that some of their sheep had longer wool than others. They would have noticed that the lambs of these particular sheep also tended to have longer wool.

 3 a Suggest why some of the sheep had longer wool than others.
   b Explain why the lambs of these sheep also had longer wool.

The farmers made use of this observation. They chose a **ram** (male sheep) with long wool. They kept the **ewes** (female sheep) away from all the other rams, and only allowed the ewes with the best wool to mate at all. This way, the lambs that were born would be likely to have longer wool.

This process was repeated time and time again, generation after generation. Eventually, the sheep that were kept looked quite different from the wild sheep. The farmers had produced a new variety of sheep.

This process is called **selective breeding**. In selective breeding for animals:

• The breeder notices that some of his animals have a variation that he would like all of them to have.
• He chooses a male and female which both show this variation.
• He breeds these animals together.
• He allows the offspring to become adults, and then once again chooses a male and female that have the feature he wants.
• He breeds these animals together.
• He goes on doing this for many generations.

In a similar way, over thousands of years, breeders have selected plants to produce crops yielding more grain, fruit and vegetables.

People still use selective breeding today. For example, Holstein cattle are bred to produce as much milk as possible. Farmers choose the **cows** (female) that produce the most milk, and mate these with their chosen **bull** (male). This has been happening generation after generation.

4 Bulls do not produce milk.
   a Why don't bulls produce milk?
   b Suggest how a farmer might choose a bull for breeding, if he wants to produce calves that will grow up (if they are female!) to produce a lot of milk.

5 Here are some figures showing the changes in milk production by Holstein cattle born between 1989 and 1999.

Year in which the cows were born	Average milk production per cow in kg
1989	5939
1990	5967
1991	6008
1992	6059
1993	6112
1994	6180
1995	6252
1996	6321
1997	6377
1998	6436
1999	6464

a Describe the trend in milk production in Holsteins, between 1989 and 1999.
b How much more milk, on average, did a Holstein cow born in 1999 produce compared with a cow born in 1989?
c Why do farmers want to breed cows that produce more milk?
d Can you think of any disadvantages of breeding cows to produce more and more milk?
e Apart from its genes, what else might affect the quantity of milk produced by a cow?

Sometimes, breeders might want to produce an animal or plant that combines two different useful characteristics. For example, they might want to breed a rose with yellow petals and good scent. They could choose as one parent, a rose with really yellow petals but not much scent, and a red rose with an excellent scent as the other parent. If they are lucky, some of the offspring might inherit the yellow colour from one parent and a good scent from the other.

This plant breeder is removing the anthers from the flowers. The anthers make the male gametes, so by doing this he stops the flowers from fertilising themselves. Later he can collect pollen from different flowers and put it onto the stigmas of these flowers to fertilise them.

Dolly the sheep

Dolly was the most famous sheep in the world. She was born in Scotland on July 5th 1996. She was famous because she was the first mammal to be **cloned** from an adult animal.

Dolly.

Cloning means producing a group of animals or plants which all have exactly the same genes. Dolly had exactly the same genes as her parent. She and her parent were genetically identical.

Some ordinary body cells were taken from a Finn Dorset ewe and grown in a laboratory. Then some egg cells were taken from a Scottish Blackface ewe. The nuclei were removed from the egg cells. One of the body cells was placed beside one of the egg cells with no nucleus and a tiny electric current was passed through them. This made the body cell and the egg cell fuse together.

The cell that was formed was not really a zygote, because it was not formed from an egg and a sperm – but it behaved like one. It divided over and over again and formed a little group of cells which grew into an embryo. The embryo was then placed into the uterus of a Scottish Blackface ewe, where it grew into a lamb in the normal way.

The research team that produced Dolly had tried many times before they were successful. They produced 277 fused body cells and egg cells, but only 29 of these developed into normal embryos. Of these 29, only one – Dolly – grew successfully into a lamb.

Since Dolly was born, many other cloned mammals, including mice, have been produced. Cloning is still very difficult and there are many failures for each success. Even when a young cloned animal has successfully been produced, it is often unhealthy. As yet, no-one has managed to clone a human. In any case, this is illegal in many countries.

Dolly died on February 14th 2003.

a Explain the meaning of each of these words.

> cloning   genetically identical   zygote

b Explain why your cells contain genes from both of your parents.

c Dolly's cells contained genes from only one parent. Was this a Finn Dorset ewe, or a Scottish Blackface ewe? Explain your answer. (You will need to read the third and fourth paragraphs carefully.)

d Explain why Dolly was a Finn Dorset sheep, even though she grew in the uterus of a Scottish Blackface ewe.

e Suggest why the egg cell had to be fused with another cell before it would grow into an embryo.

f Do you think cloning animals is a good idea? Can you think of any advantages of it? Can you think of any disadvantages?

g Do you think that, if it became possible to clone humans, this should be made legal?

Key ideas

Now that you have completed this chapter, you should know:

- that genes are made of DNA and are found on chromosomes in nuclei of cells

- that animals and plants inherit one set of genes from each of their two parents

- how identical and non-identical twins are produced

- why humans use many different varieties and breeds of plants and animals

- what selective breeding means, and how it is carried out

- what is meant by cloning, and how Dolly the sheep was produced.

Key words

bull	genes
chromosomes	identical twins
clone	non-identical twins
cow	ram
DNA	selective breeding
environment	variation
ewe	zygote
gametes	

End of chapter questions

1 These words are jumbled up. Sort each one out, then write down the name and its description, chosen from the list below.

tzoeyg   encol   tsmgeae   vilseetce   amr

a A group of genetically identical organisms.
b This kind of breeding is used to produce a variety of animal or plant with a particular set of desired characteristics.
c A male sheep.
d The cell formed when a sperm and an egg fuse together.
e Another name for sperm cells and egg cells.

2 Angela keeps Siamese cats. She wants to breed cats with especially light-coloured coats. Explain what she should do to achieve this.

3 Some sheep are kept to give milk, rather than wool. Their milk is often used to make cheese.

Awassi sheep are kept in Israel. They are good at coping with the hot, dry conditions there. East Friesian sheep are kept in Holland and Belgium. They have the highest average milk yield of any breed of sheep.

Breeders in Israel tried breeding the Awassi sheep with East Friesian sheep. They produced a new breed called the Assaf. Here is some information comparing the Awassi and Assaf breeds kept in Israel.

Characteristic	Awassi	Assaf
Average number of lambs successfully reared by each ewe each year	1.16	2.07
Quantity of milk produced in one year in kilograms	203	287

a Suggest why Israeli farmers do not keep East Friesian sheep, even though they produce more milk than Assaf sheep.
b Explain, using the information above and also what you know about genes, why Assaf sheep produce more milk than Awassi sheep.
c Can you suggest a link between the number of lambs reared by a ewe, and the quantity of milk that she produces?

4 Make a poster to illustrate the special characteristics of one rare breed of animal, explaining why you think this breed should not be allowed to die out.

5 Imagine you lived ten thousand years ago. Your family are hunter-gatherers. You have just had the idea of trying to round up some wild sheep and keeping them close to where you live. Explain to your family what you want to do, and why it is a good idea.

7 Gravity and space

What is gravity?

Why do objects fall? How fast do they fall? In which direction do they fall?

The answers to these questions will help us understand the movements of the **planets**, **moons** and **asteroids** that, together with the **Sun**, make up our **Solar System**. In this chapter we investigate one of the most important forces in science, the force of **gravity**.

According to legend, after the scientist Sir Isaac Newton saw an apple fall in his orchard in about 1665, he developed a theory about gravity. This theory explained not only the behaviour of objects falling on Earth, but also the movements of the planets.

Newton suggested that all objects were attracted to all other objects by forces he called **gravitational forces of attraction**. Sometimes, such as when you fall, you are being attracted to the Earth by quite a large force. On other occasions, for example when you stand next to a tree, the force of attraction between you and the tree is so small that you are not aware of it. Why do these forces vary so much?

Newton said that the size of these forces depended upon two things:

• the masses of the objects
• the distance between the objects.

You studied **mass** in Year 7. Mass is a measure of how much 'stuff' an object contains.

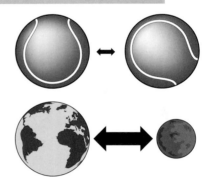

These objects both have small masses. The gravitational attraction between them is extremely small.

These objects have large masses. The gravitational attraction between them is large.

If we increase the distance between these two objects, the attraction between them decreases.

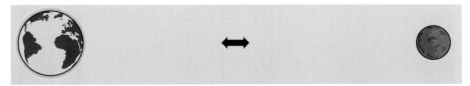

When the man on page 88 jumped from his window, he was pulled downwards by gravity – he was *attracted* by the Earth. If he had lived on the opposite side of the Earth, he would also have been pulled downwards. In fact, wherever he was on the Earth, he would be pulled down – towards the centre of the Earth.

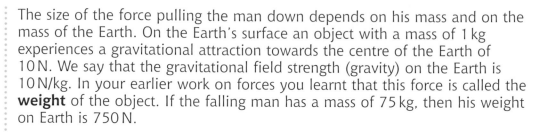

Mass and weight

YOU MAY BE ABLE TO DO WORKSHEET G1, 'MASS AND WEIGHT'.

The size of the force pulling the man down depends on his mass and on the mass of the Earth. On the Earth's surface an object with a mass of 1 kg experiences a gravitational attraction towards the centre of the Earth of 10 N. We say that the gravitational field strength (gravity) on the Earth is 10 N/kg. In your earlier work on forces you learnt that this force is called the **weight** of the object. If the falling man has a mass of 75 kg, then his weight on Earth is 750 N.

1 Why does an apple fall downwards from a tree?
2 Calculate the size of the gravitational force between the Earth and an object of mass:
   a 10 kg   b 50 kg   c 100 g (0.1 kg)

The mass of the Moon is only one-sixth that of the Earth's mass. So, if we went to the Moon, our weight would be only one-sixth that on the Earth.

The mass of the planet Jupiter is much greater than the Earth's mass. Our weight there would be approximately 2.7 times larger than that on the Earth.

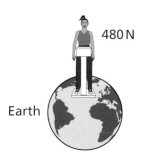

Earth — 480 N   Moon — 80 N   Jupiter — 1300 N

YOU MAY BE ABLE TO DO WORKSHEET G2, 'MASSES AND WEIGHTS ON DIFFERENT WORLDS'.

It is an important fact that, if we could travel from the Earth to the Moon or to Jupiter, our weights would change but our masses would not.

The higher you go the easier it becomes

This photograph shows the SS Discovery as it begins its flight into space. At the start of the journey the rocket is carrying a lot of fuel and so is very heavy. Its engines have to work really hard against the pull of gravity. They must produce a force greater than the weight of the rocket to make it take off. However, once the rocket begins to climb, its acceleration increases rapidly. This happens for two reasons:

• as the rocket climbs higher and higher, the pull of gravity becomes smaller
• as the rocket uses up its fuel, it becomes much lighter.

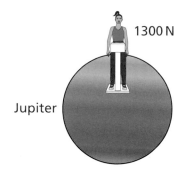

3 A man has a mass of 60 kg and a weight of 600 N. What would be the mass and weight of the man on the surface of the Moon?

4 Give one reason why it would be a good idea to launch rockets from the tops of high mountains.

5 A rocket weighs 110 000 N on the Earth. Its engines produce a total thrust of 100 000 N. Will the rocket be able to take off:
   a from the Earth
   b from the Moon
   c from the planet Jupiter?
   Explain each of your answers.

Our Solar System

People have always been fascinated by the night sky. For thousands of years they have observed the movements of the Sun, the planets and the Moon. They have tried to explain these movements by creating simple models of our Solar System. Some ancient Greek philosophers, including Ptolemy, Socrates and Plato, suggested one of the earliest models. In this **geocentric model**, the Earth was placed at the centre of the universe. The Sun, the planets and the Moon were then thought to be moving round the Earth in circular **orbits**.

> YOU MAY BE ABLE TO DO WORKSHEET G3, 'PLANETS IN OUR SOLAR SYSTEM'.

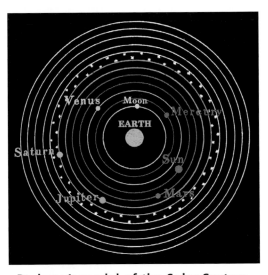

Ptolemy's model of the Solar System.

Ptolemy's model was accepted for over a thousand years until in the 16th century, a Polish astronomer named Nicolaus Copernicus suggested a new model which was able to explain the movements in the sky of the planets more accurately than Ptolemy's model. Copernicus' **heliocentric model** placed the Sun at the centre of the Solar System, with the planets, including the Earth, following circular orbits round it.

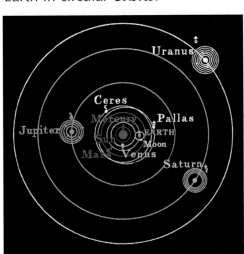

The Copernican model of the Solar System.

But even this model was not capable of describing completely accurately all the motions of the planets. Just 100 years later, in the 17th century, a German astronomer named Johannes Kepler suggested small changes to the Copernican model in order to improve its accuracy. He suggested that the orbits of the planets were not circular but **elliptical** – their paths looked like slightly squashed circles.

Elliptical planetary orbits.

6 Why did scientists make changes to the models of the Solar System proposed by Ptolemy and Copernicus?

7 What changes were made to Ptolemy's model?

8 What changes were made to the Copernican model?

Moving in a circle

This sledge is running out of control. If no forces are applied to it, it will continue to travel in a straight line and crash into the house. To change the direction of the sledge so that it misses the house, the man must pull on the rope – he must apply a force to the sledge.

Newton had studied all kinds of motion and came to the conclusion that if no forces were applied to a moving object, then that object would continue on in a straight line.

This athlete is making a heavy metal ball travel in a circle. To do this he must pull on the wire and apply a constant force to the ball so that its direction keeps changing.

9 What would happen to the ball if the wire snapped? Explain your answer.

Newton knew that the planets and their moons do not travel in straight lines – they travel in ellipses or circles. For this to happen they must be experiencing a force. But there are no wires attached to these objects, so what force is making them follow these paths? It must be gravity! The planets are held in elliptical orbits around the Sun because of the gravitational attraction between each of the planets and the Sun.

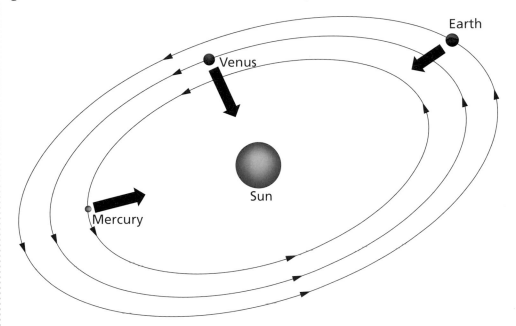

Moons travel in circular orbits around planets because of the gravitational attraction between them and their planet.

Satellites

The Moon is a **natural satellite** of the Earth. It is made to travel in a circular orbit by the Earth's gravitational pull.

We have just one moon, but some planets have several. Mars has two moons, Jupiter has 16 and Saturn has 21.

There are many other satellites orbiting the Earth but these are man-made or **artificial satellites**. Most of us make use of satellites several times each day. Do you know when you are using a satellite?

Communications satellites

Communications satellites allow us to send radio, telephone, television and internet messages to all parts of the world. Signals are sent from a transmitter up to a satellite in a fixed position above the Earth. These signals are then sent back down to the Earth or passed on to other satellites, which then send the signal to another part of the Earth.

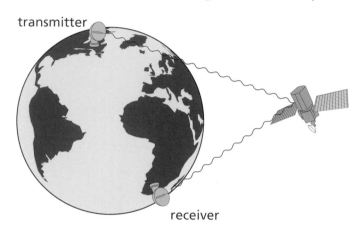

transmitter

Satellite receives signals, then sends them back to Earth or on to another satellite.

receiver

Weather satellites

This photograph shows a storm system in the Atlantic Ocean off Florida, USA. It was taken by a weather satellite high above the Earth's surface. The pictures from the weather satellite provide information to help make weather forecasting more reliable.

Hurricane Floyd.

Monitoring the whole surface of the Earth

Satellites are often used to survey the whole surface of the Earth. The information they provide helps us to assess changes in the temperature of the oceans or to monitor the crops being grown in different countries.

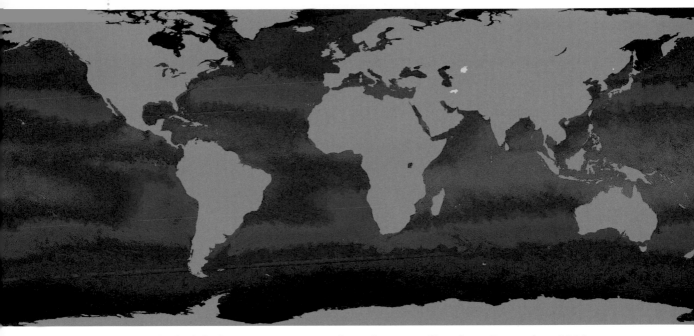

A computer model of global sea temperatures based on satellite data, December 2001.

Looking away from the Earth

Some satellites are used to look deep into outer space. The Hubble telescope shown here has enabled us to see many new objects in space which are not visible from the Earth's surface.

The Hubble Space Telescope.

Hubble Space Telescope image of light from an exploding star.

Orbiting the Earth

Artificial satellites can be put into any one of a number of different orbits. Which orbit we choose depends on how the satellite is to be used.

Weather satellites and communications satellites are often put into **geostationary orbits**. They are usually high above the Equator and travel round the Earth at the same rate as the Earth spins. As a result, these satellites stay above the same part of the Earth the whole time.

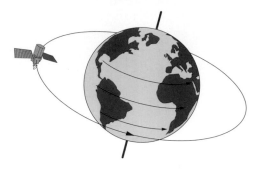

A geostationary orbit.

A low polar orbit.

In order to survey the whole surface of the Earth, a satellite is put into a **low polar orbit**. As the satellite travels between the poles, the Earth spins below it. In this orbit, a satellite scans a different strip of the Earth on each orbit and can scan the whole surface of the Earth in less than 24 hours.

10 a What is a satellite?
  b Explain the difference between a natural satellite and an artificial satellite.
  c What force keeps an artificial satellite orbiting the Earth?
  d Name two different types of orbit that a satellite may follow round the Earth.

How the Solar System began

We believe that our Solar System began as a huge cloud of dust and gases in space. Gravitational forces between the particles in the cloud gradually pulled them very close together.

This compression caused the temperature of the cloud to increase so much that nuclear reactions between hydrogen atoms began to take place in the centre of the cloud. These reactions released huge amounts of energy in the form of heat and light. This highly concentrated mass, emitting heat and light energy, is what we call a star. Our Sun had been formed.

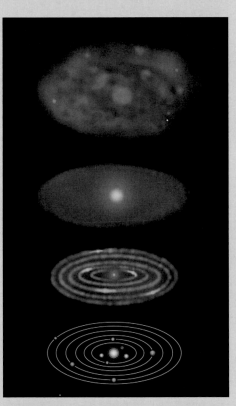

The dust and gas particles that were drawn together are also thought to have formed a thin disc shape, which then started to rotate. Smaller concentrations of dust and gases gathered some distance from the centre and eventually these became the planets and moons of our Solar System.

Between the orbits of Mars and Jupiter there is a belt of asteroids. These asteroids are pieces of rock which are orbiting the Sun and they vary in size from just a few metres to about 100 km in diameter.

No one is certain how the asteroid belt was formed. Some scientists believe that the rocks are the building blocks for a planet that never formed, but others believe that the rocks are the remains of a planet which had formed but was then torn apart by the gravity of Jupiter, the largest planet in our Solar System.

a Explain why the particles of dust and gas came together to form the Sun.
b What kinds of reactions started when the particles were highly compressed, and what did these reactions produce?
c Explain how the planets and moons of our Solar System were formed.
d What are asteroids?
e Explain how scientists think the asteroid belt may have been created.

Key ideas

Now that you have completed this chapter, you should know that:

- there are gravitational forces of attraction between objects

- the gravitational attraction between two objects increases if the mass of either object increases or the distance between the objects decreases

- an object falls because of gravity, which is the attraction between the Earth and the object

- weight is a measure of the gravitational attraction between an object and the Earth

- on other planets and on the Moon, the weight of an object will be different from that on the Earth

- over thousands of years people have put forward several different models of our Solar System to explain the movements of the Sun, Moon and planets

- a force is needed to make an object travel in a circle or an ellipse

- gravitational forces between the planets and the Sun keep the planets in orbit

- the Moon is a natural satellite

- we use artificial satellites for communications, to observe events taking place on the Earth and to look away from the Earth into outer space.

Key words

artificial satellite	mass
asteroid	moon
ellipse	natural satellite
geocentric model	orbit
geostationary orbit	planet
gravitational attraction	satellite
gravity	Solar System
heliocentric model	Sun
low polar orbit	weight

End of chapter questions

1 Rearrange these anagrams, and then write each word with its description.
  a iobtr   The path followed by a planet round the Sun
  b seiellp   A slightly squashed circle
  c eeiiolccnthr   A model of the Solar System which has the Sun at the centre
  d vaiyrgt   An attractive force between two objects
  e leiseatlt   An object which orbits a planet
  f onom   A natural satellite

2 Are these statements true or false?
  a The force of attraction between two objects increases as the two objects are moved closer together.
  b The mass of an object on the Moon is only one-sixth its mass on the Earth.
  c If no forces are being applied to an object it will travel round in a circle or an ellipse.
  d It would be easier to launch a rocket from the Moon than from the Earth as the Moon has a smaller mass.
  e A satellite in a geostationary orbit remains above one point on the surface of the Earth.
  f We measure mass in kilograms and weight in newtons.

3 Copy and complete these sentences.
  a An object anywhere on the Earth always falls _____ .
  b An average sized apple has a mass of 100g or 0.1kg. Its weight on the Earth is _____ .
  c The first models of our Solar System had the _____ at its centre. These models are called _____ models. Now we believe that the _____ is at the centre of our Solar System. This model is called a _____ model.

4 a Describe the motion of an object that is moving, but is experiencing no forces.

b Explain how the model aircraft shown in this diagram is made to travel in a circle.

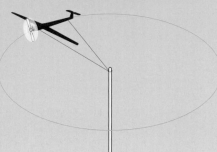

c Explain why the planets in our Solar System follow elliptical (almost circular) orbits.

5 a What is a geostationary orbit?

b Why is it an advantage to put a weather satellite into a geostationary orbit?

6 Some cars now have a GPS (Global Positioning System). Find out what this does and how it works.

7 a Explain in your own words the difference between the weight of an object and its mass.

b Imagine you are a visitor from a planet which has twice the gravitational pull of the Earth. Describe how you would notice this difference and how it might affect you.

8 Find out how satellites are placed in orbit round the Earth.

8 Using chemistry

Hot stuff

An oxyacetylene torch is being used to weld a section of the Uregol-Ushgorod oil and gas pipeline in Russia.

This man is using an oxyacetylene torch to join two pieces of metal together. But how does this torch work?

Oxyacetylene torches use a mixture of two gases – acetylene, sometimes called ethyne, and oxygen. Acetylene is a **fuel**, so when it burns it releases lots of heat energy. All things combine with oxygen when they burn. About one-fifth of normal air is oxygen. Acetylene would burn in the air but by mixing acetylene with oxygen, it burns even hotter.

The high temperature produced by the oxyacetylene torch allows the two metals to be welded together.

What chemical reactions take place when fuels burn?

In Year 7 you learnt that fuels are substances that can be burnt to release energy.

Each of these diagrams shows a fuel being used. What is each fuel and why is it being used? For example, the barbecue uses heat energy from the charcoal to cook food.

Many types of fuel are burnt to release energy. When fuels are burnt, a chemical reaction called **combustion** takes place.

When magnesium is burnt, we see an exciting chemical reaction as the magnesium burns with a brilliant white flame. The magnesium reacts with oxygen in the air to form a new compound called magnesium oxide.

The word equation for this reaction is:

magnesium + oxygen → magnesium oxide

When fuels burn they react with oxygen to form new compounds. The wax of a candle is an example of a fuel. Candle wax contains the elements hydrogen and carbon. Compounds that contain only hydrogen and carbon are called **hydrocarbons**.

When a candle is burnt, the carbon and the hydrogen in the wax react with the oxygen in the air. Provided there is a good supply of oxygen, the carbon in the candle reacts with the oxygen to form an **oxide** of carbon called **carbon dioxide**.

The word equation for this reaction is:

carbon + oxygen → carbon dioxide

The hydrogen in the candle wax also reacts with oxygen to form an oxide of hydrogen called dihydrogen oxide, which we call water vapour. We can represent this reaction using the word equation:

hydrogen + oxygen → water vapour

This diagram shows some apparatus used to test the gases produced when a candle is burnt. The candle's flame is yellow because it still contains unburnt carbon, and this shows as a small amount of black substance on the funnel. The black substance is soot.

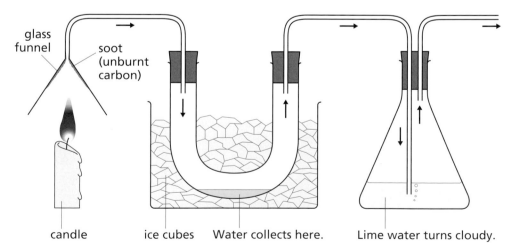

glass funnel   soot (unburnt carbon)

candle   ice cubes   Water collects here.   Lime water turns cloudy.

Soot is sometimes produced when fuels are burnt. It shows that not enough oxygen reaches the fuel for it to burn properly. This situation is known as **incomplete combustion**.

Incomplete combustion of fuels is undesirable for several reasons:

- Since some carbon is not being burnt, the flame is not as hot as it could be and so is much less efficient at heating.
- The unburnt carbon forms soot, which has to be cleaned off.
- The incomplete combustion of carbon may also produce the gas **carbon monoxide**. Carbon monoxide is a colourless and odourless gas, and is extremely poisonous. Many deaths are caused by carbon monoxide every year. People living in homes with faulty gas appliances and poor ventilation are particularly at risk.

1 Hydrocarbons are compounds that contain only hydrogen and carbon. Predict the compounds made when a hydrocarbon is burnt.

Matches

A quick and safe way to light a fire is to use a match. Matches are used so often that we rarely give them a second thought. However, striking a simple match is a good example of a combustion (or burning) reaction. A match consists of a short piece of wood or cardboard with a head at one end. The chemicals in the match head include **potassium chlorate**, sulfur and carbon.

To light a safety match, the head of the match has to be struck against the side of the matchbox which has a specially prepared rough surface. The friction caused by dragging the head of the match along the side of the box is enough to produce a flame. As the match head burns, the potassium chlorate reacts to produce the gas oxygen. The oxygen allows the other materials in the match to burn more strongly. This means that matches can be lit even in windy or damp conditions.

The other important chemicals in the match head are sulfur and carbon. These are the main fuels in the match head. As they burn they release heat energy. These fuels burn very well because of the oxygen produced by the potassium chlorate. The main part of the match is usually made of wood. Wood is a flammable material that also burns, so you have to be careful not to burn your fingers.

2 a Name two elements found in match heads.
  b Explain how striking a safety match can produce a flame.
  c Why is the compound potassium chlorate used in matches?
  d Name the two main fuels found in match heads.

How else are chemical reactions used as energy resources?

We know that when a fuel burns, energy is released. Apart from combustion reactions of fuels, how else are chemical reactions used as energy resources?

In Chapter 4, you studied the thermit reaction. This is an example of a **displacement reaction**: aluminium displaces the iron in iron oxide, to produce iron and aluminium oxide. The equation for the reaction is:

aluminium + iron oxide → aluminium oxide + iron

This reaction produces lots of heat energy, so much, in fact, that the iron produced is molten.

Chemical reactions that produce electrical energy

During many chemical reactions energy is given out as heat, but energy can be released in other ways. Some chemical reactions can release energy in the form of *electricity*.

A simple electrical cell can be made when two different metals are pushed into a fruit. In this diagram, strips of iron and copper are pushed into an orange.

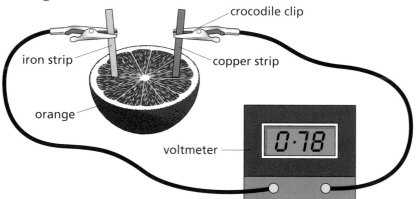

A cell changes chemical energy into electrical energy, which the current carries round a circuit. The amount of this energy is measured as the **voltage** of the cell. (See page 162 for more about voltage.)

The voltage of the cell is an indication of the energy being produced by the chemical reaction, and can be measured by connecting the two metals to a voltmeter.

Chapter 4 explains that metals may be placed into an order of reactivity. This order is used to predict which pair of metals would make a battery producing the highest voltage.

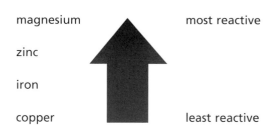

magnesium — most reactive
zinc
iron
copper — least reactive

This cell has been made using a strip of magnesium and a strip of copper.

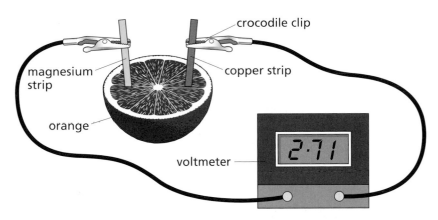

YOU MAY BE ABLE TO DO WORKSHEET H2, 'CHEMICAL REACTIONS AS ENERGY RESOURCES'.

How does the energy produced depend on the reactivity of metals?

When magnesium and copper are used to make a cell, more energy is released than when iron and copper are used. There is a greater difference in reactivity between magnesium and copper than there is between iron and copper.

> The greater the difference in reactivity between the two metals used in the cell, the greater the energy released, and the higher the voltage produced by the cell.

3 Lead is less reactive than copper. Cell A contains magnesium and lead. Cell B contains magnesium and copper. Which cell produces the higher voltage?

More displacement reactions

When a metal such as magnesium or zinc is added to a copper sulfate solution, a colour change shows that a chemical reaction is taking place. This is another example of a displacement reaction.

When magnesium is added to copper sulfate solution, the more reactive magnesium displaces the less reactive copper from the copper sulfate solution. The word equation for the reaction is:

magnesium + copper sulfate → magnesium sulfate + copper

4 Write a word equation for the reaction between zinc and copper sulfate solution.

During both chemical reactions there is also a temperature change. The size of the temperature change depends on the difference in reactivity between the metal added and the metal in the metal sulfate solution.

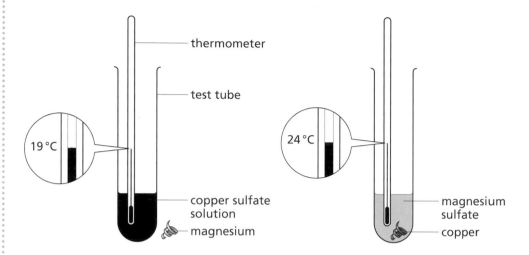

5 Describe the temperature change when magnesium is added to copper sulfate solution.

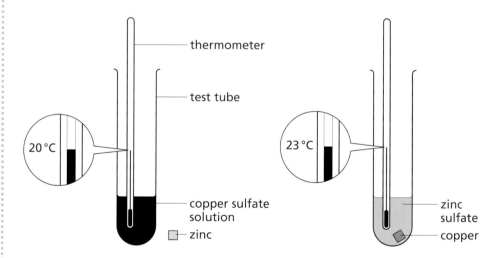

6 Describe the temperature change for the reaction when zinc is added to copper sulfate solution.

7 Which variables must be controlled to allow a fair comparison to be made between these two experiments?

The greater the difference in reactivity between the two metals, the greater the energy released, and the greater the temperature change during the reaction.

Self-heating cans

The energy produced by chemical reactions can be useful in different ways. You may have seen some self-heating drinks cans in supermarkets. These cans have two sections. For example, liquid coffee is stored in the top part of the can, while the bottom section of the can contains two chemicals, calcium oxide (quicklime) and water. A thin layer of foil separates the quicklime and the water from each other. When the bottom of the can is pushed, the foil is broken, so the water comes into contact with the quicklime. The two chemicals react, and heat is released which warms up the coffee. This invention uses a chemical reaction that allows people to drink hot coffee wherever they are.

Coffee product

insert

foil separator

quicklime

plastic button

water

How are new medicines developed?

The **medicines** – also known as **drugs** – that are prescribed by doctors were all developed by groups of scientists. Every day in this country, the pharmaceutical industry invests over £8 million into researching and developing new medicines.

The team of scientists who are researching treatment for a particular disease makes a list of chemicals that could be useful as medicines. Up to ten thousand new chemicals can be investigated at this stage.

For example, suppose the aim is to help people who suffer from asthma. The researchers first discover what happens when someone has an asthma attack. They compile a list of chemicals that might stop airways from constricting and causing breathing difficulties for asthma sufferers. They then use computers to model how they think each chemical will react, and they also carry out tests on cell cultures in the laboratory. These tests will eliminate nearly all of the original list of potential medicines.

In the next stage, scientists use animals to test the chemicals that they think will work. The bodies of most mammals work in very similar ways. If the chemicals do not damage the bodies of animals, then the researchers can predict that the chemicals will probably also be safe for people. They also need to work out how much of each chemical to use as a medicine.

Only after all this research has been successfully completed, can scientists give the chemicals to healthy volunteers to check that the chemicals really are safe for humans. If a chemical proves to be safe, the regulatory authority allows it to be used as a medicine in **trials** on real patients. If the medicine works and is safe, the regulatory authority can grant a licence.

Only when the medicine is licensed can it be sold. Some of the money from the sale of the medicine will be used to start research into new medicines. All these steps can take a very long time. It usually takes about ten years for a new medicine to reach the market.

What happens to the atoms when new materials are made?

When you studied chemical reactions in Year 7, you learnt how to tell that a chemical reaction is taking place by observing what happens.

When silver nitrate solution is added to sodium chloride solution, a white **precipitate** is made. This precipitate is called silver chloride.

> A precipitate is an insoluble solid formed when two solutions are mixed together.
>
> The formation of a precipitate tells us that a chemical reaction has taken place.

The word equation for this reaction is:

silver nitrate   +   sodium chloride   →   silver chloride   +   sodium nitrate
(colourless solution)   (colourless solution)   (white precipitate)   (colourless solution)

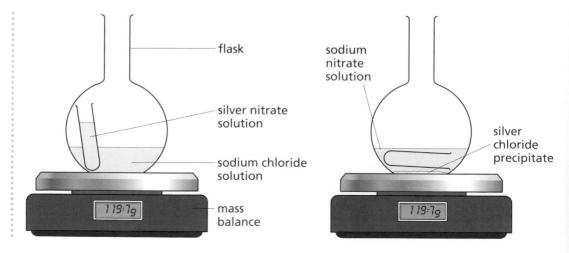

When an iron nail is added to copper sulfate solution, a displacement reaction occurs.

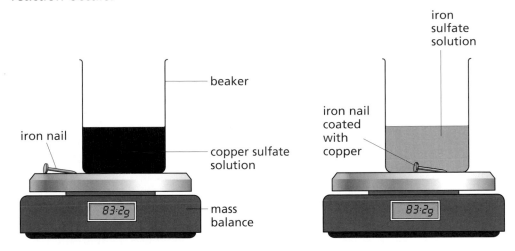

8 a Write a word equation for this displacement reaction.
  b Explain how you can tell that a chemical reaction has occurred.

When the alkali sodium hydroxide is added to hydrochloric acid, there is a change in temperature. This tells us that a chemical reaction has taken place. The hydrochloric acid neutralises the alkali, so this can be described as a **neutralisation reaction**.

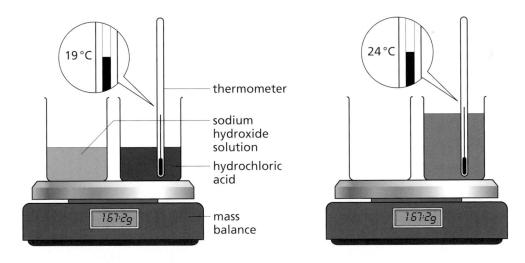

9 a Write a word equation for this chemical reaction.
  b What indicator has been used in this experiment?
  c Calculate the temperature change in this reaction.

In all these chemical reactions, *the total mass before* and the *total mass after* the reaction are the *same*. New substances are made, but they are made from the substances that were already there. No atoms are being made or destroyed – they are just being combined in different ways.

Using a model to explain what happens during a chemical reaction

When a hydrogen balloon explodes, the hydrogen burns and there is a very loud and exciting chemical reaction. The hydrogen in the balloon reacts with the oxygen in the air. This is what happens to the atoms during the chemical reaction.

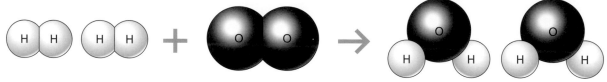

2 molecules of hydrogen

Each molecule of hydrogen contains two hydrogen atoms.

join with 1 molecule of oxygen

The oxygen molecule contains two oxygen atoms.

to form 2 molecules of water

Each molecule of water contains one oxygen atom and two hydrogen atoms.

No atoms are made or destroyed during this reaction. The atoms are just rearranged so that they are joined together in a different way. This means that the total mass before and the total mass after the reaction are the same.

What happens when gases are produced during a chemical reaction?

When a metal such as magnesium is added to hydrochloric acid, bubbles of a gas are produced. These bubbles show that a chemical reaction is taking place.

The equation for this reaction is:

magnesium + hydrochloric acid → magnesium chloride + hydrogen

If the reaction flask is placed on a mass balance, the mass of the flask and its contents appears to decrease slightly over time. This is because one of the **products** of this chemical reaction is the gas hydrogen. As some of the hydrogen escapes into the air, the flask and its contents become lighter. The hydrogen produced has mass, but because it has escaped into the air, the flask and its contents have a lower mass.

Even when a chemical reaction produces a gas, the *total mass before* and *after* a reaction is the *same*.

What happens when a substance dissolves?

Unlike the other changes we have examined in this chapter, **dissolving** is a physical change. When salt crystals are placed in water the salt dissolves. The solution made is colourless. The salt is still there, even though we can no longer see it.

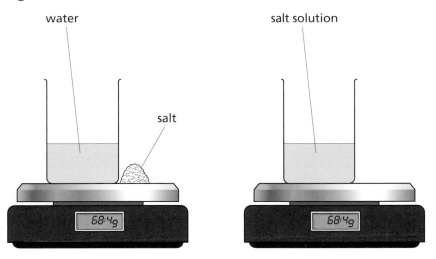

The mass of the salt and the water before the salt dissolves in the water and the mass after the salt dissolves in the water are the same.

> The total mass before and the total mass after all physical changes are the same.

Burning magnesium

When magnesium is burnt, there is a chemical reaction. The magnesium reacts with oxygen in the air and the compound magnesium oxide is made. But does the mass of the magnesium change as it reacts?

To find out, we need to measure the mass of the magnesium before the reaction and the mass of the magnesium oxide after the reaction. Magnesium oxide is a white powder which can easily be blown away and so spoil the results. To prevent this happening, we use a crucible – a small pot with a lid. Crucibles are usually made of ceramics or metals and must be able to withstand very high temperatures.

First, the mass of the crucible is recorded. The magnesium is then put in the crucible and the lid is replaced, and the total mass of the crucible and the magnesium is noted.

The crucible containing the magnesium is heated fiercely and eventually the magnesium begins to burn. As the magnesium burns, the lid of the crucible is lifted occasionally and carefully replaced. Lifting the lid allows oxygen in the air to reach the magnesium so that it can burn. Replacing the lid quickly prevents any magnesium oxide from escaping.

Before the reaction

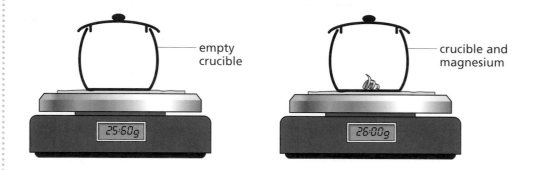

empty crucible

crucible and magnesium

mass of magnesium = (mass of crucible + magnesium) – mass of crucible

After the reaction

crucible and magnesium oxide

YOU MAY BE ABLE TO DO WORKSHEET H4, 'BURNING MAGNESIUM'.

mass of magnesium oxide = (mass of crucible + magnesium oxide) – mass of crucible

10 Copy and complete this table.

Mass of magnesium (g)	Mass of magnesium oxide (g)

The mass of the magnesium oxide is greater than the mass of the magnesium metal. This is because when magnesium metal burns, it combines with oxygen in the air (which also has mass) to produce the new compound magnesium oxide.

11 A Year 9 Science class carried out an experiment to find out how the mass changed when magnesium was burnt.

This table shows the results from each group in the class.

Group	Mass of magnesium (g)	Mass of magnesium oxide (g)
A	1.02	1.66
B	0.62	1.00
C	0.93	1.52
D	0.87	1.03
E	0.32	0.53
F	0.53	0.88

a Draw a set of axes like these.

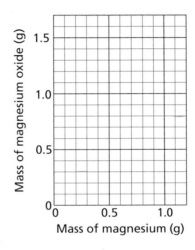

b Plot each group's result on your graph.
c Draw a line of best fit on your graph.
d Explain the relationship between the mass of magnesium and the mass of magnesium oxide produced.
e Use your graph to predict the amount of magnesium oxide that would be produced when:
   i   0.40 g of magnesium is burnt
   ii   0.65 g of magnesium is burnt
   iii 1.00 g of magnesium is burnt
f i   Which group's results are lower than expected?
   ii   Suggest a possible reason for this.

Burning bread

The molecules from which bread is made include starch. Starch is a carbohydrate, the molecules of which contain carbon, hydrogen and oxygen.

When bread is burnt, chemical reactions take place and new substances are made. The carbon atoms in the bread combine with oxygen atoms to form the compound carbon dioxide.

The word equation for this reaction is:

carbon + oxygen → carbon dioxide

The hydrogen atoms in the bread combine with oxygen atoms to form water vapour. The word equation for this chemical reaction is:

hydrogen + oxygen → water vapour

If the carbon and hydrogen atoms are combining with oxygen atoms, then why does the mass of the bread go down?

The carbon dioxide and the water vapour produced during this chemical reaction are both gases. These gases (which have mass) escape into the air, so the mass of the bread goes down.

What would happen if the carbon dioxide and water vapour made during the reaction could be collected?

If the toast is burnt inside a sealed container, then the gases produced during the reaction cannot escape. As expected, the total mass before and the total mass after the reaction are the same.

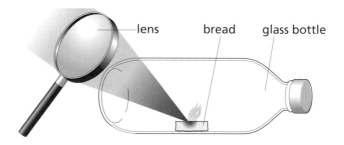

During all chemical and physical reactions, the total mass before and the total mass after the reaction are the same.

The greenhouse effect

Although there is only a small amount of carbon dioxide in the Earth's atmosphere, it has an enormous effect on the climate.

The Earth absorbs heat energy from the Sun, becomes warm and emits some of its own energy back into outer space. Some energy is unable to escape, as it is absorbed by carbon dioxide molecules in the atmosphere. As the amount of carbon dioxide in the atmosphere increases, less of the energy emitted by the Earth can escape, so the Earth and its atmosphere become warmer. This phenomenon is called the greenhouse effect – the carbon dioxide traps heat in much the same way as glass traps heat in a greenhouse.

Without some carbon dioxide in the atmosphere, most of the rays emitted by the Earth would escape and the temperature at the Earth's surface would be below the freezing point of water. Our oceans, seas and rivers would all be frozen and life would not exist.

However, if the amount of carbon dioxide in the atmosphere dramatically increases, the Earth could become like the planet Venus. The atmosphere of Venus is about 95% carbon dioxide. Venus experiences a kind of 'super-greenhouse effect', which means that the surface temperature of Venus is about 450 °C – too hot for life to exist.

Since the Industrial Revolution, people have burnt increasing amounts of the fossil fuels coal, oil and gas. So, over the past two hundred years, the levels of carbon dioxide in the atmosphere have gradually increased.

Scientists believe that even a small increase in the amount of carbon dioxide in the atmosphere could cause changes in weather patterns. This could lead to droughts and storms which would dramatically affect both agriculture and water supplies.

Environmental groups have been concerned about the long-term effects for our planet of a rise in carbon dioxide levels, and have urged research into alternative energy resources such as wind farms. However, while the world's poorest countries are probably most vulnerable to environmental problems, it is the world's richest countries who are the world's worst polluters. Rich countries are likely to resist plans to reduce the amount of carbon dioxide they produce, if it means that their economies are badly affected.

a What would happen if there was:
  i no carbon dioxide in the Earth's atmosphere
  ii a lot more carbon dioxide in the Earth's atmosphere?
b Write a letter to your local MP explaining why there should be more research into alternative energy resources in your area.
c One possible source of energy is from the nuclear industry. Find out about the advantages and disadvantages of the nuclear industry.

Key ideas

Now that you have completed this chapter, you should know:

- that fuels burn to release energy
- that when fuels containing hydrogen are burnt, water vapour is produced
- that when fuels containing carbon are burnt in plenty of oxygen, carbon dioxide is produced – if there is not enough oxygen for the fuel to burn properly, carbon and carbon monoxide are also produced
- how to evaluate the advantages and disadvantages of different fuels
- how to apply knowledge and understanding of combustion to the everyday context of burning matches
- that during a chemical reaction, no atoms are made or destroyed – the atoms are merely arranged in a different way – so mass does not change
- some of the stages in the development of new products.

Key words

carbon dioxide	medicine
carbon monoxide	neutralisation reaction
combustion	oxide
displacement reaction	potassium chlorate
dissolve	precipitate
drug	product
fuel	trial
hydrocarbon	voltage
incomplete combustion	

End of chapter questions

1 Are these statements true or false?
  a New materials are made during a chemical reaction.
  b The total mass before and the total mass after a chemical reaction are the same.
  c During chemical reactions atoms are made and destroyed.
  d Chemical reactions often release heat energy.
  e When carbon is burnt a new compound known as water is made.

2 Rearrange these anagrams and then write out the word or words with the correct description.
  a ebanoncodmorix
  b tipcparteie
  c aruatoosicpmhtsle
  d rtawe pavrou
  The compound formed when hydrogen is burnt in air.
  A chemical used in match heads, which releases oxygen and so allows other materials to burn better.
  A dangerous compound formed when carbon is burnt in a limited supply of oxygen.
  An insoluble product when solid made when two solutions react.

3 Copy and complete these word equations.
  a magnesium + oxygen → _____
  b copper + oxygen → _____
  c sodium hydroxide + sulfuric acid → _____ + _____
  d potassium hydroxide + nitric acid → _____ + _____
  e copper sulfate + magnesium → _____ + _____
  f zinc + iron sulfate → _____ + _____

4 The word equations represent six different chemical reactions. Each reaction has a letter. We can place chemical reactions into different groups. The table shows four different groups of reaction. Complete the table by placing the letter representing each reaction into the correct group.
  A carbon + oxygen → carbon dioxide
  B copper + silver nitrate → copper nitrate + silver
  C calcium carbonate → calcium oxide + carbon dioxide
  D sulfuric acid + calcium hydroxide → calcium sulfate + water
  E silver chloride → silver + chlorine
  F aluminium + oxygen → aluminium oxide

Neutralisation reaction	Displacement reaction	Combining with oxygen (oxidation reaction)	Other reaction

5 These descriptions show the key stages in the development of a new medicine, but the steps are out of order.
Put the sentences in the correct order to explain how the medicine is made.

A Scientists research a particular disease and make a list of chemicals that could be useful as medicines.

B Scientists give the chemicals which appear to work to healthy volunteers. They must check that the chemicals are safe to use on humans.

C Only when the medicine is licensed can it be sold.

D Scientists use computers to model how they think the chemical will react. They also carry out tests on cell cultures in the laboratory.

E If the medicine is safe, the regulatory authority allows the chemical to be used in trials on patients.

F Scientists test the chemicals on animals. They need to know that the drugs will not harm the animals.

G Some of the money from the sale of the medicine will be used to start research into new medicines.

H If the medicine works and is safe, the regulatory authority can grant a licence.

6 Solve each clue and then find the answer in the wordsearch.

a A fuel found in match heads.

b Another word for combustion.

c The gas found in air which is needed for combustion.

d A material which can be burnt to release heat.

e A chemical change.

s	b	l	e	u	f	o	s
x	i	u	o	x	x	o	u
s	m	k	r	y	u	c	l
h	d	c	g	n	z	j	f
v	p	e	f	m	i	o	u
t	n	h	b	m	l	n	r
g	k	a	f	x	o	n	g
r	e	a	c	t	i	o	n

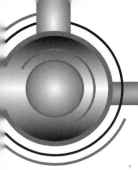

9 Plants and photosynthesis

Can you imagine the world without plants?

There would be no oxygen to breathe ...

... and there would be nothing to eat.

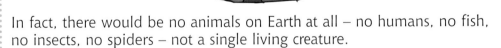

In fact, there would be no animals on Earth at all – no humans, no fish, no insects, no spiders – not a single living creature.

It is difficult to appreciate how important plants are. They seem to just exist and never do anything very exciting. They do not sing, jump about, swim around or bite you. So what is it that they do that is so very important?

To really find out what a plant is doing, you would need to shrink to the size of a molecule and look right inside its cells. There you would see an incredible process taking place. This process is something that you could never do, but it is so amazing that plants do not need to 'do' much else. All they have to do is sit in the sun.

What plants can do that you – and all other animals in the world – will never be able to do is **photosynthesise**.

Photosynthesis

'Photo' means something do to with light. (Think about photographs, for example.) 'Synthesis' means 'making'. So photosynthesis means 'making with light'.

The substance that plants make by photosynthesis is **glucose**. Glucose is a carbohydrate and is an important source of energy for all living things. Using glucose as an energy source and a raw material, plants are able to make all the other materials from which their bodies are made. And, from these, animals obtain all the materials from which *their* bodies are made, too.

The raw materials for photosynthesis

A green plant is like a factory, using raw materials to make a useful product. A plant needs just two raw materials for making glucose. These are:

- **Carbon dioxide** Plants get their carbon dioxide from the air. Only a tiny proportion, 0.03%, of the air is carbon dioxide, so plants are very clever at obtaining it. Later, we will see how their leaves are adapted for extracting carbon dioxide from the air very effectively.

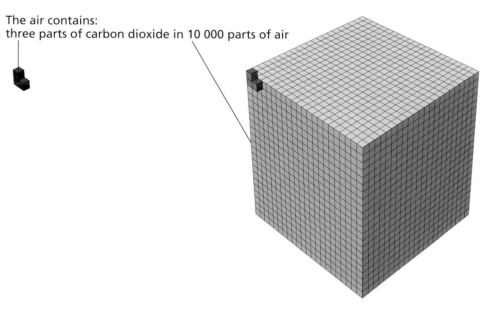

The air contains:
three parts of carbon dioxide in 10 000 parts of air

- **Water** Plants get their water from the soil through their roots. Later, we will see how a plant's roots are adapted for extracting water from the soil.

YOU MAY BE ABLE TO DO WORKSHEET I1, 'HOW DOES PHOTOSYNTHESIS AFFECT CARBON DIOXIDE CONCENTRATION?'.

The energy supply for photosynthesis

YOU MAY BE ABLE TO DO WORKSHEET 12, 'WHICH PARTS OF A VARIEGATED LEAF CONTAIN STARCH?'.

As with most manufacturing processes, the manufacture of glucose from these raw materials needs an energy supply. The energy that plants use is the energy in **sunlight**.

Green plants are able to use this energy because they contain a green substance called **chlorophyll**, found in the **chloroplasts** inside some of the plant's cells. Chlorophyll absorbs energy from sunlight, and then this energy is used for photosynthesis.

Imagine you were full of chlorophyll. You could simply stand in the sun and photosynthesise. In fact, some animals have set up a close relationship with plants so that they can do just that. The little animals that make coral, for example, are miniature sea anemones, which allow tiny plant cells to live inside their bodies. The plants photosynthesise and provide the coral animals with carbohydrates.

Why do you think coral reefs can only grow where the sea is fairly shallow?

The products of photosynthesis

YOU MAY BE ABLE TO DO WORKSHEET 13, 'OXYGEN PRODUCTION BY A PHOTOSYNTHESISING WATER PLANT'.

We have already seen that one of the products of photosynthesis is glucose. Glucose is a carbohydrate. Its molecules contain some of the energy from the sunlight that reaches the plant.

The other product of photosynthesis is **oxygen**. During the daytime, when sunlight is falling on them, plants make and release oxygen. In fact, plants have made almost all of the oxygen in the air around us. When the Earth was very young, before plants evolved, there was no oxygen in the atmosphere at all.

The photosynthesis equation

YOU MAY BE ABLE TO DO WORKSHEET 14, 'HOW DOES LIGHT INTENSITY AFFECT THE RATE OF PHOTOSYNTHESIS?'.

We can summarise the process of photosynthesis with a simple word equation:

$$\text{carbon dioxide} + \text{water} \xrightarrow[\text{by chlorophyll}]{\substack{\text{energy absorbed} \\ \text{from sunlight}}} \text{glucose} + \text{oxygen}$$

This woodland is a peaceful place. Who would imagine that it is a massive carbohydrate factory?

Do plants need soil to grow?

We almost always see plants growing in soil. Not surprisingly, before scientists understood about carbon dioxide, photosynthesis and so on, they thought that plants grew because they absorbed soil. Now we know that they do not. In fact, one of the most modern and efficient ways of growing plants for food does not use soil at all. Instead, the plants grow with the roots suspended in water. This method is called **hydroponics**.

Plants become heavier as they grow because of all the carbon dioxide and water they have absorbed. The molecules of carbon dioxide and water combine to make glucose. Later, the plant can turn this glucose into other substances, such as cellulose for its cell walls.

These lettuces are growing with their roots in moving water, not in soil.

However, as you will see later, plants do need *something* from the soil. They take in tiny quantities of minerals such as nitrates and potassium. If you are growing plants hydroponically, you need to add these to their water supply. The amounts of minerals are minute compared with the amount of carbon dioxide and water that the plants use.

Leaves, roots and photosynthesis

The different parts of a plant help it to obtain what it needs for photosynthesis. The leaves and roots are especially important for this.

Leaf structure

YOU MAY BE ABLE TO DO WORKSHEET 16, 'THE STRUCTURE OF LEAVES'.

The leaves are the 'factory floor' of the plant, where the glucose is made.

The structure of a leaf is adapted so that photosynthesis can take place really fast. This means the cells have plenty of the raw materials and energy that they need.

The leaf is very thin, so the sunlight can get right inside to reach the cells where photosynthesis happens.

The broad, flat surface of the leaf gives it a very large surface area, so lots of sunlight and carbon dioxide reach it.

There are tiny pores on the underside of the leaf which allow carbon dioxide to diffuse into the leaf.

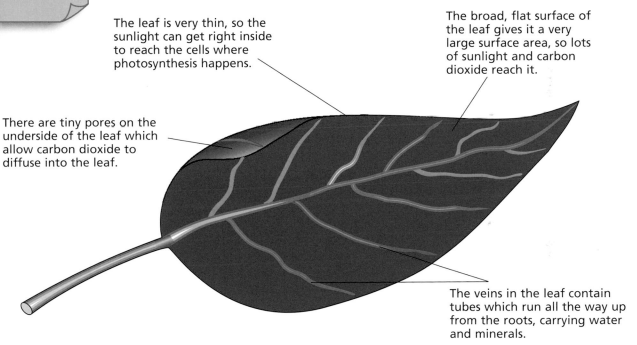

The veins in the leaf contain tubes which run all the way up from the roots, carrying water and minerals.

1 Copy and complete this table to summarise how a leaf is adapted to obtain the raw materials and energy that it needs for photosynthesis.

What is needed for photosynthesis	How a leaf is adapted to get plenty of it
carbon dioxide	
water	
sunlight	

Inside a leaf

If you cut a leaf in two, and look at it edge-on using a microscope, you will see something like this.

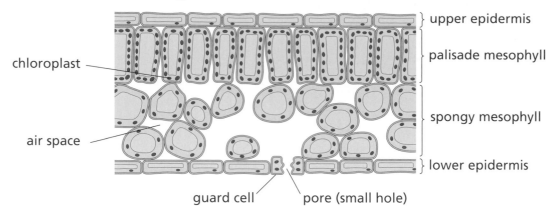

chloroplast

air space

} upper epidermis

} palisade mesophyll

} spongy mesophyll

} lower epidermis

guard cell   pore (small hole)

There are several different kinds of **cells** in the leaf. The cells are arranged in layers, with similar cells in each layer. Each group of similar cells is called a **tissue**.

2 a How many different tissues can be seen in the leaf?
  b Which three kinds of cells can photosynthesise? Why do you think this?
  c Carbon dioxide gets into the leaf through the small holes on the underside. Why might having air spaces inside the leaf help photosynthesis to happen faster?
  d Give three reasons why you can tell that the cells in the diagram are all plant cells, not animal cells.

YOU MAY BE ABLE TO DO WORKSHEET 17, 'THE CELLS IN A LEAF'.

Roots

The roots of a plant soak up water from the soil. The water is carried in tubes up to the leaves. The leaf cells need water to use in photosynthesis.

A tree's root system may be as big as the parts you can see above the ground. These roots have been exposed by a landslip.

YOU MAY BE ABLE TO DO WORKSHEET 18, 'THE STRUCTURE OF ROOTS'.

Roots are well adapted for their function of absorbing water. They grow down into the soil, probing between the tiny soil particles into the spaces where water is found.

The tip of a root is covered with a protective layer, so the living cells behind it are not damaged as they push through the soil.

Behind this, the root grows hundreds of tiny **root hairs**. They give the root a very large surface area. This helps water to pass into the root really quickly, because there are so many root hairs that can all absorb water at the same time.

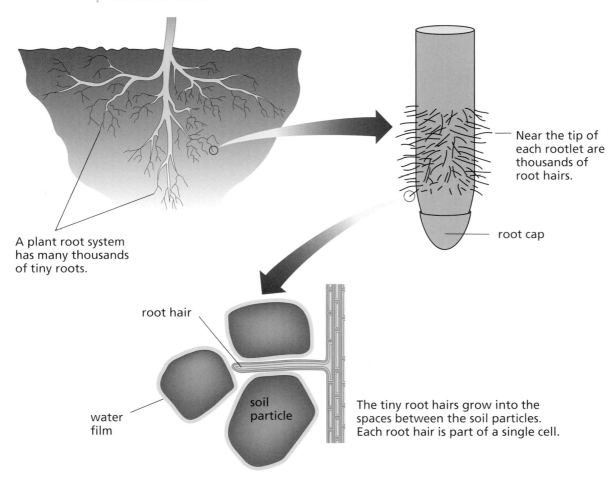

A plant root system has many thousands of tiny roots.

Near the tip of each rootlet are thousands of root hairs.

root cap

root hair

water film

soil particle

The tiny root hairs grow into the spaces between the soil particles. Each root hair is part of a single cell.

3 Just like all living cells, the cells inside roots need to respire.
   a Why do all cells need to respire?
   b There are air spaces in the soil. Which gas do roots absorb from these air spaces?
   c Which gas do the roots release into the air spaces?

Plants and the environment

Photosynthesis and food for animals

As a plant photosynthesises, it becomes heavier, because it uses the glucose it makes to produce new bits of plant.

The glucose can be made into many different chemicals:

- **Starch** is stored by the plant for use as an energy source later on.

- **Cellulose** forms cell walls. When a plant is growing, it is producing many new cells. They all need a cell wall, and this uses up a lot of the glucose.

- **Proteins** and **fats** help to build the plant's cells, or can be stored away to be used later on.

Food for animals

All of the substances made by a plant provide food for animals when they eat the plant. All of the substances contain energy, which originally came from the sunlight that reached the plant.

4 Not all animals eat plants. So how does photosynthesis help to provide food for a carnivore such as a tiger?

Photosynthesis and oxygen

When plants photosynthesise, they take in carbon dioxide and release oxygen.

Plants help to keep the concentration of carbon dioxide in the atmosphere quite low, and they help to keep the concentration of oxygen in the atmosphere high.

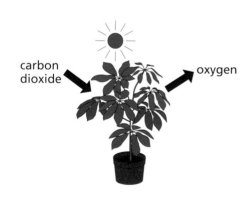

carbon dioxide

oxygen

YOU MAY BE ABLE TO DO WORKSHEET 19, 'HOW DO PLANTS AFFECT THE OXYGEN CONCENTRATION IN A POND?'

Animals depend on this oxygen. The animals living in a pond use oxygen that is dissolved in the water. Some of this oxygen comes in from the air, through the surface of the water, but a lot of it comes from plants. If you watch the water-weed in a pond on a sunny day, you can often see the bubbles of oxygen coming out of its leaves.

Biosphere 2

On September 26th 1993, four women and four men walked out of a huge glass and steel building in the Arizona desert for the first time in two years. They had been taking part in a project called Biosphere 2, living in a completely closed and airtight environment to find out if people and plants could survive in the building with no inputs or outputs of food or gases. They did – but not without some problems along the way.

It had been hoped that the carbon dioxide and oxygen levels in the atmosphere would stabilise, because of a balance between photosynthesis and respiration in the living organisms inside the building. However, from the start there were problems with carbon dioxide levels soaring much higher than they should be. The cause was eventually tracked down to the much larger than expected population of bacteria in the soil, which were feeding on the waste material that was there. At one stage, the carbon dioxide level was eight times higher than in normal air. The organisers of the project had to put a carbon dioxide 'scrubber' into the building for a few weeks, to chemically remove some of the carbon dioxide from the atmosphere.

The eight people had to grow their own food. Their diet was mostly based on the plants they grew. They also kept pigs for meat, chickens for eggs and goats for milk. The waste from the people and the animals was recycled to provide nutrients to help the plants to grow.

There were occasional food shortages. Although Arizona can usually rely on having bright, sunny weather, during the Biosphere 2 project there were unexpectedly cloudy winters and these led to crop failures. This also contributed to the problem of falling oxygen levels. Extra oxygen had to be supplied to the building on two occasions.

Nevertheless, all eight people emerged at the end of the two years looking reasonably healthy. Perhaps most importantly, apart from one broken teacup, which one of them had thrown at a colleague, they had managed to live without any serious conflict.

a Give two reasons why it was important to have lots of plants inside the Biosphere 2 building.

b Explain how 'a balance between photosynthesis and respiration' should have kept the carbon dioxide and oxygen levels constant.

c Suggest what process was happening in the soil bacteria, that resulted in the high carbon dioxide concentration building up.

d Explain why the 'unexpectedly cloudy winters' led to:
  i crop failures
  ii falling oxygen levels.

e Imagine you are one of the organisers of the Biosphere 2 project. Write an advertisement, to go into a magazine of your choice, to recruit potential 'survivors' for the next two years of the project.

Key ideas

Now that you have completed this chapter, you should know:

- that plants make glucose and oxygen by photosynthesis
- that they do this by combining carbon dioxide with water inside the cells in their leaves
- that sunlight is needed to provide energy for photosynthesis
- that chlorophyll in the leaf cells absorbs sunlight so that it can be used in photosynthesis
- how to write the word equation for photosynthesis
- that plants store some of the glucose they make as starch
- how to test a leaf for starch
- how plants affect the concentration of carbon dioxide and oxygen around them
- that animals depend on plants for food and oxygen
- that plants increase their mass when they photosynthesise
- how a leaf is adapted to help photosynthesis to happen
- how palisade cells are adapted for photosynthesis
- how roots are adapted to absorb water.

Key words

carbon dioxide	oxygen
cell	palisade cells
cellulose	photosynthesis
chlorophyll	proteins
chloroplasts	root hairs
epidermis	starch
fats	sunlight
glucose	tissue
hydroponics	

End of chapter questions

1 Unjumble each of these words and match them with their definitions.

thlig   sirha   dsplaiea   pesritoniar
lhpycolholr   xgyneo   sgceluo   reatw

a A carbohydrate made in plants when they photosynthesise.
b The green pigment (colour) in plants that absorbs sunlight.
c Cells in a leaf which are tall and thin, and contain many chloroplasts.
d Tiny extensions on a root which give it a large surface area for soaking up water.
e The gas which plants release when they photosynthesise.
f The substance which is combined with carbon dioxide during photosynthesis.
g A process which happens inside the cells of all living things, in which energy is released from glucose.
h The energy needed for photosynthesis.

2 A gardener grows carrots. Some of her carrots grow in a shady part of the garden, and some grow in a sunny part.
a Suggest why the carrots in the sunny part of the garden grow larger than the carrots in the shady part.
b The gardener is not sure that the carrots are different because some grow in the sun and some in the shade. What other reasons could there be for the differences between them?

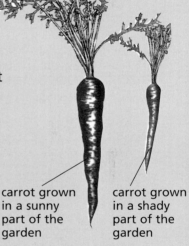

carrot grown in a sunny part of the garden

carrot grown in a shady part of the garden

3 a Arrange these statements in order, to describe how you test a leaf for starch.
A Drop some iodine solution onto the leaf.
B Put the leaf into boiling water for a few minutes.
C Put a tube of alcohol into the beaker of hot water.
D Dip the leaf into water to soften it.
E Put the leaf into the hot alcohol, so that the chlorophyll comes out of it.
F Spread the leaf out carefully on a white tile.
b If the leaf contains starch, what colour would you expect to see when you have finished the test?
c If the leaf does not contain starch, what colour would you expect to see when you have finished the test?

4 All living organisms respire. Animals and plants respire all the time.
  a Name the gas which animals and plants take in when they respire.
  b Name the gas which animals and plants give out when they respire.
Plants can also photosynthesise. They only photosynthesise when it is light. They photosynthesise faster than they respire.
  c Name the gas which plants take in when they photosynthesise.
  d Name the gas which plants give out when they photosynthesise.
  e Which gas do you think plants give out during the night? Explain your answer.
  f Which gas do you think plants give out during the daytime? Explain your answer.

5 A water plant was placed in a sealed container of water. The concentration of carbon dioxide in the water was measured for a 24-hour period. This graph shows the results.

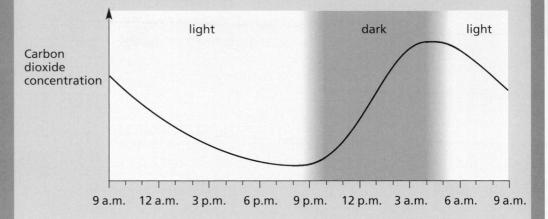

  a At what time of day was the carbon dioxide concentration lowest?
  b Explain why the carbon dioxide concentration was low at this time.
  c At what time of day was the carbon dioxide concentration highest?
  d Explain why the carbon dioxide concentration was high at this time.
  e The daytime measurements were made on a dull, rainy day. Suggest what difference there might be in the results if the experiment was done again on a bright, sunny day.

6 Design a poster showing one of these:
  • Why we need plants
  • How leaves and roots are adapted for their functions

10 Plants for food

A lot of the food that we eat comes from plants. Sometimes it is obvious that you are eating part of a plant, for example, a lettuce leaf or a tomato. Sometimes it is less obvious, because the plant product has been processed to look very different from when it was growing.

1 All of these foods are parts of plants. For each one, name the part of the plant that it has come from. Choose from:

leaf   fruit   seed   tuber   root   bulb

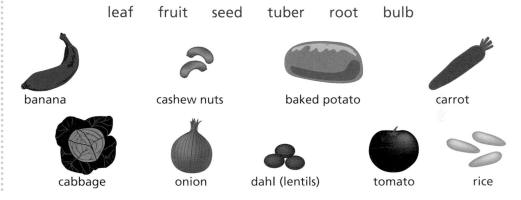

banana   cashew nuts   baked potato   carrot

cabbage   onion   dahl (lentils)   tomato   rice

Photosynthesis and food production

Plant foods contain a whole range of different nutrients. They can contain carbohydrates (starch and sugar), protein, fat, vitamins and minerals. Of these, all but the minerals have been made inside the plant's cells.

First, the plant made glucose by photosynthesis.

carbon dioxide + water $\rightarrow$ glucose + oxygen

Then it used the glucose to make the other types of nutrients.

Plants do not make these nutrients for our needs; they do it for themselves.

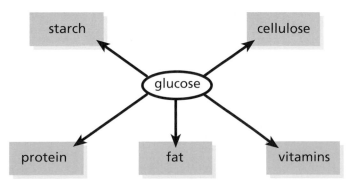

YOU MAY BE ABLE TO DO WORKSHEET J2, 'TESTING DEFFERENT PARTS OF PLANTS FOR STARCH'.

They use all of these nutrients to grow and to reproduce.

For example, what happens when a plant reproduces? It grows flowers, which produce nectar to attract insects, which will pollinate them. The nectar contains sugars, such as glucose and fructose (fruit sugar). After the flower has been pollinated, seeds grow inside its ovaries. Each seed contains a tiny embryo plant. The seed contains food stores to keep the embryo plant alive until it has grown into a young plant that can photosynthesise for itself. These food stores often include starch, fat and protein.

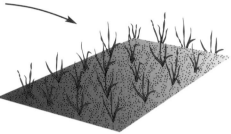

Wheat seeds are sown in autumn.

The grain is taken away to make flour and other foods. Some grain is kept to sow in the autumn.

The seeds germinate and grow into young plants. The plants stay small all through the winter.

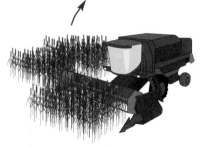

In late summer, the grain is ripe and can be harvested.

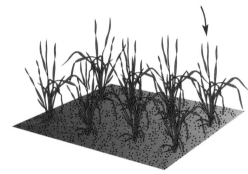

In spring, as it gets warmer, the wheat plants start growing again.

The pollinated flowers produce seeds. The seeds are known as grain.

In summer, the wheat plants produce flowers. The flowers are pollinated by the wind.

2 a Explain why the wheat plants do not grow during the winter months.

b The mass of the grain that the farmer harvests is much greater than the mass of the seed that he sowed. Where has this extra mass come from?

c Wheat grains (seeds) contain a lot of starch and protein. What is the advantage to wheat plants of having these nutrients in their seeds?

Fertilisers

People who grow plants for food, either to eat themselves or to sell, usually want their plants to produce a lot of nutrients as quickly as possible. They try to give the plants what they need to grow fast and strong, and to photosynthesise really well.

For photosynthesis, all that a plant needs is carbon dioxide and water, plus plenty of sunlight. With these, it can make glucose, and starch from the glucose.

Glucose and starch, like all carbohydrates, have molecules made of just three different kinds of atoms – carbon, hydrogen and oxygen.

However, protein molecules contain another kind of atom – **nitrogen**. So, to make some of the glucose into proteins, plants need small amounts of nitrogen. They obtain nitrogen in the form of **nitrate**. Plants absorb the nitrate they need for making proteins from the soil.

YOU MAY BE ABLE TO DO WORKSHEET J4, 'HOW DOES NITRATE AFFECT THE GROWTH OF DUCKWEED PLANTS?'.

Large and vigorous plant with dark green leaves.

Short and weak plant with yellowish leaves.

A barley plant grown with plenty of nitrogen.

A barley plant grown without nitrogen.

Nitrate is an example of a **mineral** that plants absorb from the soil. Plants also need small amounts of other minerals, including **potassium** and **phosphorus**, for healthy growth. Farmers often test their soil to find out whether it contains enough of the different minerals that their crops need. If it does not, then they apply **fertilisers** to the soil.

There are many different kinds of fertilisers. Farmers can use bags of granular fertilisers made by large chemical companies, or they can use waste materials such as manure from cattle, which contain minerals, including nitrates, that plants can use.

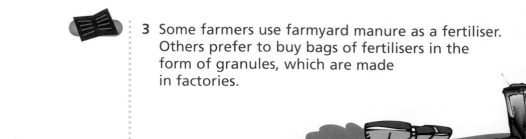

3 Some farmers use farmyard manure as a fertiliser.
Others prefer to buy bags of fertilisers in the
form of granules, which are made
in factories.

    a Suggest as many reasons as you can why some farmers choose to
apply farmyard manure as a fertiliser.
    b Suggest as many reasons as you can why some farmers choose to
apply granular fertilisers.

4 This bag contains fertiliser.
The letters are the symbols of the elements
that are contained in the fertiliser. What
are the three elements?

Weeds

Weeds are plants that are growing where they are not wanted. For
example, if a farmer has a field of wheat, then he does not want any other
plants growing in the field. Other plants growing amongst the wheat plants
are weeds.

Why weeds reduce yields

A lot of weeds growing amongst a crop can reduce the **yield**. The yield is
the quantity of crop that the farmer harvests.

A weedy crop of wheat may produce less grain than a crop without any
weeds. This happens because the weed plants need the same things as the
wheat plants. They **compete** with the wheat for light, carbon dioxide,
water and minerals. If the wheat plants get less of these things, then they
cannot photosynthesise and grow so well, and so they produce less grain.

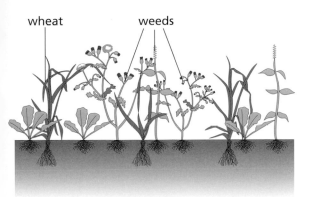

If there are too many weeds, the crop plants will not grow well.

Weed-killers

YOU MAY BE ABLE TO DO WORKSHEET J5, 'INVESTIGATING WEEDS'.

Farmers and gardeners usually try to get rid of weeds. Gardeners often pull the weeds up one by one, but you cannot do this in a field of wheat. Many farmers spray their crops with chemicals, which kill the weeds but not the crop plants. These are called **selective weed-killers**.

A grower has to think carefully before deciding to use weed-killers. Here are some of the disadvantages and advantages of using them. You may be able to think of others.

Disadvantages

- Weed-killers are expensive, so the farmer has to work out how much they will cost, and whether he is likely to recoup this much extra money from the better crop that he will grow.
- Some weed-killers can be harmful to human health. Workers using weed-killers should wear protective clothing.
- Many insects and other animals eat the weed plants. If the weeds are killed, then these animals have no food and will no longer live there.
- The farmer cannot spray weed-killers on windy days, as he does not want the spray to drift where people will breathe it.

Advantages

- Getting rid of weeds reduces competition with the crop plants, and so may increase the yield of the crop.
- Weeds can be habitats for insects which might feed on the crop plants, or pass diseases on to them.
- When the farmer harvests a crop of wheat, he does not want weed seeds mixed in with the wheat grains, as this would make rather peculiar flour. It would also reduce the price he can expect for his wheat.

5 An experiment was carried out to discover if removing weeds from fields of beans increased the yield of beans. A large field was sown with bean seeds. The field was marked out into ten equal-sized squares. In the first week, the weeds were removed from Square 1. In the second week, the weeds were removed from Squares 1 and 2. In the third week, the weeds were removed from Squares 1, 2 and 3, and so on for ten weeks.

This graph shows the results of the experiment.

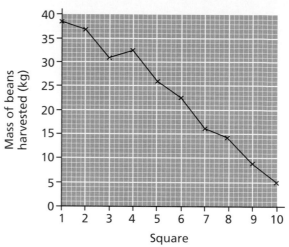

a Which square gave the greatest yield of beans?
b Which square had weeds in it for the greatest length of time?
c Complete this sentence to describe the trend shown by the results.
   The longer the time that weeds were allowed to grow amongst the bean plants, the _____ the yield of beans.
d Suggest an explanation for these results.
e Suggest a reason for the unexpected result in Square 4.

How to be a good weed

It is not easy to be a weed. Weeds have to be able to survive even though people try to get rid of them. These diagrams show two examples of plants that have adapted to survive as weeds.

Low growing rosette of leaves escapes mowing or being eaten.

Flowers produce large numbers of fruits which parachute off to new places.

Plant grows very rapidly so it can produce seeds before anyone gets round to killing it off or pulling it up.

If you try to pull up the plant, the deep root just breaks off and grows into a new plant.

Dandelion growing in a lawn.

Groundsel growing in a crop of wheat.

Pests

A crop pest is an animal that damages a crop and reduces the yield. Many pests are insects that feed on the crop plant.

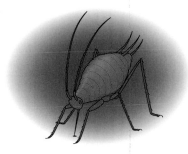

Aphids (greenfly) suck sap from wheat plants.

Leafhoppers eat the leaves of rice plants.

Carrot fly larvae eat carrot roots.

Growers often spray chemicals onto their crops to kill insect pests. These chemicals are called **pesticides**. If the pesticide is meant to kill insects, then it is an **insecticide**. Like herbicides, pesticides can be dangerous to humans, so great care must be taken when using them.

In how many ways is this man protecting himself from the pesticide he is spraying on the tomatoes?

Harmful effects of pesticides

Unfortunately, pesticides often have harmful effects on many different animals, not only the pest. For example, if you spray a pesticide onto a rose bush to kill **aphids**, you will probably kill bees and ladybirds too. Bees and ladybirds do not do any harm at all – in fact, both of them are useful to gardeners. Bees pollinate flowers, while ladybirds are predators that eat aphids.

Another way that pesticides can be harmful is by affecting food webs.

6 This is part of a food web in a garden.

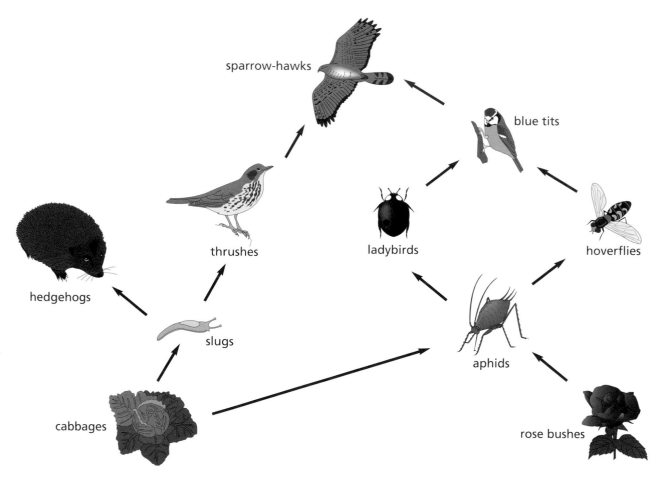

sparrow-hawks

blue tits

thrushes   ladybirds   hoverflies

hedgehogs

slugs

aphids

cabbages   rose bushes

a Explain how using a pesticide to get rid of the slugs could affect the food web.
b Explain how using a pesticide to get rid of the aphids could affect the food web.

Persistent pesticides in food chains

Today, the pesticides that we can buy in Britain are very carefully regulated. They are all **biodegradable**. This means that they break down very quickly after they have been used, so they only have short-term effects.

Not all pesticides are biodegradable; some of them are **persistent**. This means that they last for a long time. One example of a persistent pesticide is **DDT**.

DDT is an insecticide that was used a lot in Britain in the 1940s to 1960s. It was thought to be very safe, because tests showed that while low concentrations of it killed insects, it was only harmful to other animals in much, much higher concentrations.

However, people gradually began to realise that DDT was harming birds of prey. This was happening because the DDT did not break down. If DDT was absorbed by an insect, it stayed there. Each time a bird such as a blue tit ate an insect, it ate some DDT as well. Over its lifetime, as it ate thousands of insects, it absorbed more and more DDT, all of which stayed in its body.

Very high concentrations of DDT built up in animals at the end of food chains. There is some evidence that DDT made birds of prey, such as sparrow-hawks and peregrine falcons, produce eggs with shells that broke easily, so fewer young hatched out. Adult birds died, too. When their bodies were analysed, they were found to contain huge concentrations of DDT. The populations of the birds of prey fell rapidly.

DDT has been banned in the UK since the mid 1970s and since then the populations of sparrow-hawks and peregrine falcons have gradually grown again.

(ppm = parts per million)

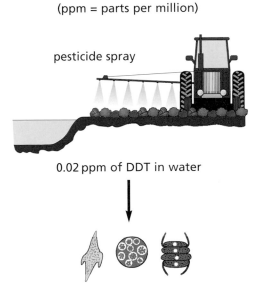

pesticide spray

0.02 ppm of DDT in water

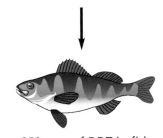

5 ppm of DDT in microscopic organisms

250 ppm of DDT in fish

1600 ppm of DDT in grebe

DDT accumulation along a food chain.

Growing crops in glasshouses

In Britain, a number of different crops are grown in **glasshouses**. The grower can control the conditions inside the glasshouse in ways that cannot possibly be done outside in a field.

Controlling the temperature

Usually, the main reason for growing crops under glass is that it would be too cold for them outside. Some of the plants grown in Britain, for example tomatoes and cucumbers, originally came from warmer parts of the world. They could not survive outside in freezing temperatures. If we grow them in glasshouses, then we can keep them warm all the time, and produce tomatoes much earlier and later in the year than if we grow them outside during our short and unpredictable summers.

Controlling light

Plants need lots of light to grow well, and inside a glasshouse, extra light can be provided. This allows the plants to grow even during the winter months, when the hours of natural daylight are short.

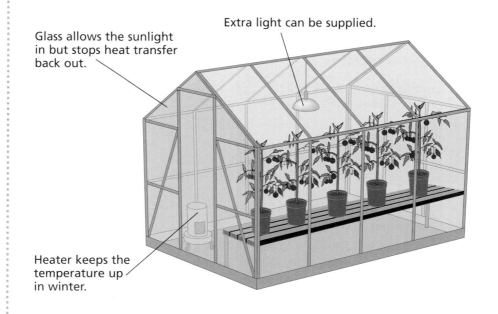

Extra light can be supplied.

Glass allows the sunlight in but stops heat transfer back out.

Heater keeps the temperature up in winter.

7 a In some glasshouses, the temperature is kept up by burning paraffin. Paraffin is a fossil fuel. What gases will it produce when it burns? How might this help the growth of the plants in the glasshouse?

b If it becomes too hot inside the glasshouse, ventilators can be opened in the roof. Explain how convection will help to cool things down.

Mosquitoes, malaria and DDT

Malaria is a very dangerous disease that kills millions of people each year, mostly in hot countries where a particular kind of **mosquito** lives. Malaria is caused by a pathogen that is carried from person to person by the mosquitoes. There is no vaccine against malaria.

DDT has been a very valuable weapon in the fight to control malaria. It is cheap, so it can be used even in poor countries. It is effective in very small concentrations, so not much needs to be used to kill a lot of mosquitoes. It is persistent, so once a house has been sprayed with DDT, no mosquitoes can live there for quite some time afterwards.

DDT is already banned in the USA and in Europe. There are plans for a global ban on DDT from 2007. Here are two views on this proposed ban.

The World Wide Fund for Nature

DDT harms wildlife. It is persistent and builds up in food chains, damaging animals at the top of the chain. Even though it is no longer used in Europe and America, if you analyse foods there, you still find it. One orchard in the USA still contained 40% of the DDT that had been sprayed onto it 20 years ago. DDT can spread huge distances; if it is sprayed in an African village it can end up in the fat of polar bears in the Arctic. It has also been found to contaminate human breast milk. We have evidence that it can affect unborn and very young children, affecting brain development. We do not need DDT. Safe alternatives can be developed.

The World Health Organisation

We need DDT. It is the only cheap, relatively safe chemical we can use in the fight against malaria. There is no alternative. All the other insecticides we have available are much too expensive to use in poor villages in countries like Guyana and Ghana. Malaria kills more than 2 million people each year. It kills one child under the age of 5 every 30 seconds. If we use DDT, we can prevent many of these deaths. The problem with DDT was that it was used carelessly and irresponsibly. There is no scientific proof that it is harmful to humans. If we take care how we use it, it can be safe. It is practically criminal not to use DDT where malaria is common. It is all very well for rich Europeans to say it should be banned – they do not have malaria in their countries, and anyway they have plenty of money to afford more expensive alternatives.

a Explain the meaning of these words:
   pathogen   vaccine   persistent   contaminated   insecticide
b Find out where Guyana and Ghana are.
c Imagine you are a reporter for a magazine. Write a balanced article explaining both sides of the argument for and against imposing a global ban on the use of DDT. Finish the article by stating your own point of view on which way the decision should go.

Key ideas

Now that you have completed this chapter, you should know:

- some examples of foods that are made from plants
- why fertilisers help plants to grow well
- how some plants are adapted to be successful weeds
- why weeds can reduce crop yields
- why pests can reduce crop yields
- how weed-killers and pesticides can affect food webs
- how glasshouses can provide the best conditions for crops to grow well.

Key words

aphid	nitrate
biodegradable	nitrogen
compete	persistent
DDT	pesticide
fertiliser	phosphorus
glasshouse	potassium
insecticide	selective weed-killer
malaria	weed
mineral	weed-killer
mosquito	yield

1 Write a short definition of each of these words, as they are used when talking about growing crops.
  a fertiliser
  b weed
  c pesticide
  d selective weed-killer
  e persistent
  f yield
  g competition

2 These diagrams show the life cycle of a potato plant. The potatoes that we eat are tubers, and they grow underground.

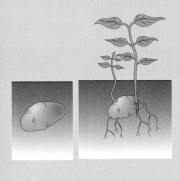
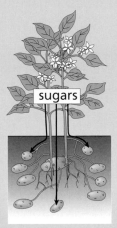
sugars
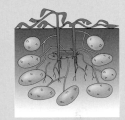

Spring A potato tuber is planted in the ground. Roots and shoots begin to grow.

Summer The plant is fully grown. Sugars made in the leaves are used to make new potatoes.

Autumn The leaves die. The potatoes are harvested and stored for the winter.

  a Potato tubers contain a lot of starch. Use the diagrams, and what you already know about how plants make carbohydrates, to explain where the starch in a potato comes from.
  b Suggest why potato plants grow leaves during the summer, but not in the winter.
  c Use the diagrams to explain why it is useful to the potato plant to store starch in its tubers.

3 No-one wants to buy carrots that have already been half eaten by carrot fly larvae, or apples with maggots in them, but many people do not want to see the environment harmed by pesticides, either. Find out about some of the ways in which growers can produce good-quality crops without using pesticides. What are the advantages and disadvantages of these pesticide-free methods?

4 A trial was carried out in New Zealand to find out how good a new weed-killer is. The weed-killer, called pine essence, is made from pine trees. The pine trees are harvested and crushed to make pulp and paper, and the weed-killer is made from the waste materials left over after this process.

An area of ground was dug over. It was left for 10 days for the weeds to germinate. Then one third was sprayed with pine essence and one third with another weed-killer called glyphosate.

Thirty days after the weed-killers had been sprayed, the weeds on a sample area of each part of the ground were collected, dried and weighed. These are the results.

Weed-killer	Mass of weed-killer used in kg per hectare of ground	Dry mass of weeds remaining in kg per hectare of ground
none	0	277
pine essence	92.5	6
glyphosate	0.51	33

a Using the description of the experiment, state three variables that the researchers kept constant in their experiment.
b Using the results table, give one way in which their experiment was not really a fair test of the effectiveness of the two weed-killers.
c Suggest a technique the researchers might have used to collect the sample of weeds from each area of ground.
d Glyphosate is an expensive weed-killer, made by the chemical industry. Suggest as many reasons as you can (apart from the fact that it might smell nicer!) why some growers might prefer to use pine essence.

5 Some farmers in the UK now use a technique called precision farming. This involves using Global Positioning Systems (GPS) and soil analysis to map out which parts of their fields need the most fertiliser.
Find out how precision farming works. What are the advantages to the farmer? Why don't all farmers use it?

6 About 64% of the food eaten in Britain is grown here. A recent survey showed that more than one third of adults do not know that cherries are grown in Britain, two thirds do not know that sugar beet is grown in Britain and one in ten thinks that we grow rice here.
Make a poster, or design a leaflet, that will help people to understand that a lot of the food they eat is grown in the British countryside.

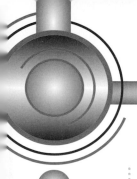

11 Environmental chemistry

On November 14th 1963, a volcano on the seabed just to the south of Iceland began to erupt. So much lava poured out and solidified that the new rocks reached right above the surface of the sea. A new island was being formed. The Icelanders named it Surtsey, after the mythical fire-giant Surtur.

Surtsey just after the eruption.

Surtsey began its life as a pile of basalt reaching to a height of 172 m above sea level. It covered $2.5 \, km^2$. Now it is less than half this size, covering an area of just over $1 \, km^2$. The basalt has weathered and then been eroded away by the fierce waves of the Atlantic Ocean crashing on to its shores.

Other changes have taken place, too. The new island was made of bare rock. Now, there is a thin layer of **soil** in some places, and on the soil there are plants – not many plants, and there is not much soil, but still this is a big change from the lifeless island that first appeared over 40 years ago.

Surtsey in 1998.

Soil

Which came first on Surtsey – the plants or the soil? The answer is that they have gradually increased together, one helping the other to develop. Most plants cannot grow until there is soil to grow in, and soil cannot develop until there are plants.

How soil forms

Rocks undergo **weathering** when they are exposed to air or water. The weathering breaks the solid rocks into small pieces. It is these small rock fragments that form the major part of many kinds of soil.

Sometimes, the rock fragments stay where they first formed, but sometimes they are carried away by water or the wind. This is called **erosion**. Eventually, these rock fragments will be dropped somewhere else – this is called **deposition**.

A few plants may begin to grow amongst the deposited rock fragments. Plants that are able to grow in these barren places are called **pioneer plants**, because they are the first ones to colonise a new area.

The pioneer plants must be able to survive harsh conditions. The deposited rock particles may move around quite a bit, making it difficult for plant roots to hang on. When it rains, the rock particles are not very good at keeping hold of water for very long, so the plants must be able to survive in dry conditions. The rock particles may not contain the minerals that the plants need – for example, on Surtsey there was hardly any nitrate in the rock.

Seagulls helped on Surtsey. They flew to the new island from Iceland, and left droppings on the rocks. Their droppings helped to supply minerals for the newly colonising plants, and to form the first thin layer of soil.

As the plants grew, bits of them fell off or died. These plant remains rotted in the soil, forming dark, sticky material called **humus**. The humus helped to hold the rock particles together and to hold water after rainfall. It also contained minerals such as nitrate, so as more humus built up, more plants could grow there. And, of course, the more plants that grew, the more the humus built up.

How soil is formed from rock particles.

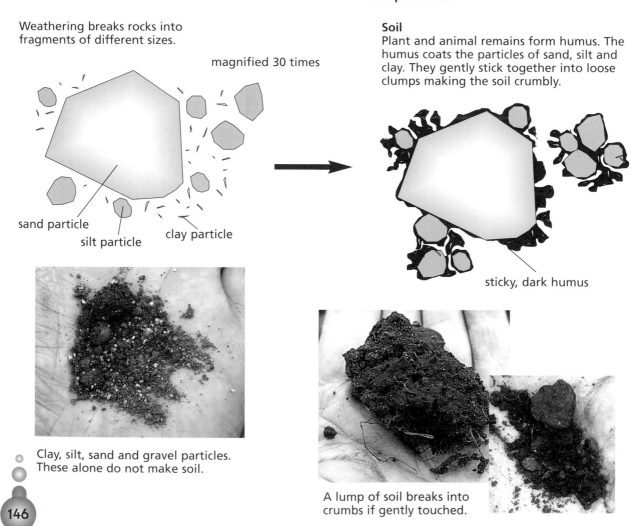

Weathering breaks rocks into fragments of different sizes.

magnified 30 times

sand particle

silt particle

clay particle

Soil
Plant and animal remains form humus. The humus coats the particles of sand, silt and clay. They gently stick together into loose clumps making the soil crumbly.

sticky, dark humus

Clay, silt, sand and gravel particles. These alone do not make soil.

A lump of soil breaks into crumbs if gently touched.

What soil contains

If you shake some soil in water and then allow it to settle, you can see some of the different things it contains.

Chalky soil **Clay soil**

dead plant material — water — clay and fine silt — silt — stones, chalky lumps, sand and silt — soil particles

— dead plant material — water — clay — clay and fine silt — silt — stones, sand and silt

- Rock fragments usually make up the bulk of the soil. They are called **soil particles** once they become part of soil. Different sizes of particles produce different kinds of soil. If there are a lot of large particles, the soil is sandy. If there are a lot of very small particles, the soil is clayey. Most soils have a mixture of particles of different sizes.

- Remains of living organisms, such as twigs, dead leaves and animal droppings, are also part of the soil. They rot down to form humus. The more humus in the soil, the better it is for plants to grow in.

- Many organisms live in the soil. You are unlikely to find a mole in a spadeful of soil from your garden, but you might find an earthworm and it will certainly be full of invisible bacteria. (There are twice as many bacteria in half a teaspoon of soil as there are people in the whole world.) Earthworms help to make good soil by dragging dead leaves down into it, eating them and passing them out of their digestive systems as faeces. This adds to the humus content of the soil. The bacteria, too, feed on plant and animal remains, releasing minerals from them that plants can use.

There is a whole world down in the soil.

Soil particles do not fit together perfectly. There are little spaces between them, which fill up with air or water. Unless the soil is very dry, there is usually a thin film of water covering each soil particle. This is the water supply for plant roots. The air in the soil is very important for providing oxygen to plant roots, soil animals and bacteria. They all need oxygen for respiration.

Soil pH

YOU MAY BE ABLE TO DO WORKSHEET K2, 'MEASURING THE pH OF SOIL'.

The kind of particles that make up a soil affects the pH of the soil. For example, if the particles came from limestone rocks, then the soil will be alkaline. Soils that form in limestone or chalk areas often have a pH of 8.

A lot of humus and decaying vegetation in a soil tends to make it more acidic, because rotting vegetation forms acids.

Most plants grow best in a neutral or slightly acid soil. This is true for most crop plants grown in Britain, such as wheat and potatoes.

1 This table shows the range of soil pH that some vegetable and herb plants need for healthy growth.

Plant	pH range
Peas	6.0–7.5
Broccoli	6.0–7.0
Carrots	5.5–7.0
Potatoes	4.5–6.0
Courgettes	5.5–7.0
Leeks	6.0–8.0
Parsley	5.0–7.0
Mint	7.0–8.0

a Which plant can grow in the most acidic soil?
b Which plants can grow in the most alkaline soil?
c Which plants have the widest range of pH in which they can grow well?
d Which plant do you think would grow least well if your garden was in a limestone area?

Altering soil pH

Farmers and gardeners often want to raise plants that do not grow well in their soil. They can try to change the pH by adding things to the soil.

If the soil is more acidic than they would like, they can try adding **lime**. Some forms of lime contain **calcium carbonate**. Calcium carbonate reacts with acids and neutralises them.

calcium carbonate + acid → calcium salt + carbon dioxide + water

If the soil is more alkaline than they would like, they can try adding **manure** to the soil. Manure adds rotting plant material to the soil, which releases acids.

2 A farmer has a large field in which he wants to grow a crop which prefers a neutral soil. He has the soil pH tested all over the field. Then he has a map made of the field showing the pH of the soil.

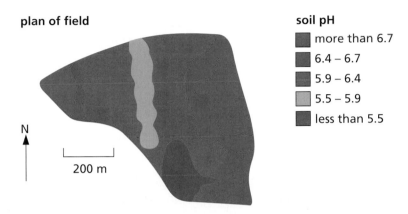

plan of field

N

200 m

soil pH
- more than 6.7
- 6.4 – 6.7
- 5.9 – 6.4
- 5.5 – 5.9
- less than 5.5

  a Suggest why different parts of the field contain soil with different pH values.

  b What can the farmer add to the soil to bring the pH closer to 7?

  c Suggest how the farmer can make use of the map to help him to do a good job for the least amount of money.

3 Jake has an allotment. He changes the crop he grows on a particular piece of ground each year, like this:

    Year 1 carrots
    Year 2 potatoes
    Year 3 broccoli
    Year 4 peas

Jake's soil has a pH of around 5.5. In which year or years should he add lime to the soil before he plants his crops? Explain your answer. (You will need to use the information in the table on page 148.)

Acid rain

Normal rain is slightly acid. It has a pH of around 5.6. This happens because the air contains carbon dioxide. Some of the carbon dioxide dissolves in the rain water and forms carbonic acid.

$$\text{carbon dioxide} + \text{water} \rightarrow \text{carbonic acid}$$

Carbonic acid is only a weak acid. Even if there is a lot of it in the rain, the pH of the rain will not fall below 5.2.

However, sometimes rain can be much more acid than this. If the pH of the rain is less than 5.0, then it is called **acid rain**.

How acid rain is formed

Acid rain forms when **sulfur dioxide** or **nitrogen oxides** dissolve in rain water. They form sulfuric acid and nitric acid – two strong acids. Sometimes, if there are a lot of these gases in the air, the rain can be extremely acid. On April 10th 1974, rain falling at Pitlochry in Scotland had a pH of 2.4. This is more acid than vinegar.

Where do these gases come from? Both of them have natural sources, but they are also produced by human activities.

Volcanoes

Coal-fired power stations

 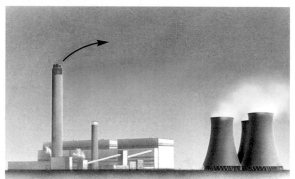

Some sources of sulfur dioxide.

Sulfur dioxide is present in the gases released by erupting volcanoes. Sulfur dioxide is also formed when some fossil fuels burn. These fossil fuels, especially coal, contain sulfur. When the fuel burns, the sulfur combines with oxygen in the air.

sulfur + oxygen → sulfur dioxide

Lightning produces nitrogen oxides in the air.

Nitrogen oxides are present in the exhaust fumes from cars and all other vehicles.

Some sources of nitrogen oxides.

You may be able to do Worksheet K3, 'Measuring the pH of rain water'.

Nitrogen oxides are formed during thunderstorms. As lightning forks through the air, the huge amounts of energy in it make nitrogen in the air combine with oxygen. This also happens inside car engines.

nitrogen + oxygen → nitrogen oxides

4 Copy and complete this table about the gases that produce acid rain.

Gas	One natural source	One man-made source	How it forms acid rain
sulfur dioxide			
nitrogen oxides			

5 Explain why carbon dioxide in the air is **not** important in forming acid rain.

How acid rain affects living organisms

YOU MAY BE ABLE TO DO WORKSHEET K4, 'INVESTIGATING THE EFFECT OF ACID RAIN ON SEED GERMINATION'.

Plants and animals can be harmed by acid rain.

Acid rain can make streams, rivers, ponds and lakes acid. This can kill fish and many kinds of invertebrates. For example, crayfish have calcium carbonate in their external skeletons. Animals cannot take up calcium from acid water, so crayfish cannot get the calcium they need to make their skeletons.

Crayfish cannot survive in acidified rivers and lakes.

Acid rain harms trees. It affects the soil in which they grow, making it more difficult for them to absorb the minerals that they need.

These trees in the Czech Republic were killed by acid rain.

6 Even very acid rain falling on soil formed from limestone does not do much harm.
 a What does limestone contain?
 b What will happen when acid rain comes into contact with limestone?
 c How will this stop the acid rain doing any harm to living things?

How acid rain affects rocks and buildings

YOU MAY BE ABLE TO DO WORKSHEET K5, 'INVESTIGATING THE EFFECT OF ACID RAIN ON BUILDING MATERIALS'.

Many kinds of rocks contain carbonates. Limestone and chalk contain calcium carbonate. In some sandstones, the 'cement' that holds the sand grains together contains calcium carbonate.

If rain contains acid, for example sulfuric acid, it will react with the calcium carbonate like this:

sulfuric acid + calcium carbonate → calcium sulfate + carbon dioxide + water

As the calcium carbonate reacts, the rock breaks down. This is an example of chemical weathering.

Even ordinary rain is slightly acid, so it will help to weather rocks containing calcium carbonate, but acid rain will do this much more quickly.

We often use rocks containing calcium carbonate for making buildings. Acid rain can cause a great deal of damage to buildings made of these kinds of rocks.

Acid rain will also react with metals. Metal structures can become badly corroded by acid rain. For example, the iron in iron railings may react like this:

iron + sulfuric acid → iron sulfate + hydrogen

Acid rain has damaged this sculpture on the roof of the Cloth Hall in Cracow, Poland.

Controlling pollution by acid rain

We cannot do anything about the natural sources of acid rain such as thunderstorms, and we cannot stop volcanoes erupting, but we can reduce the **emissions** of sulfur dioxide and nitrogen oxides that are produced by human activities.

Reducing sulfur dioxide emissions

Most of the sulfur dioxide that is emitted comes from burning coal to generate electricity in power stations.

Measures are now taken to cut down the quantity of sulfur dioxide produced.

- We can stop burning coal, and use alternative fuels such as oil or gas, which contain less sulfur.

- We can use only coal which has a low sulfur content.

- We can pass the gases produced when the coal is burnt, through 'scrubbers'. These produce a spray containing a mixture of finely ground limestone and water, through which the gases have to pass before they go out into the air. This removes the sulfur dioxide.

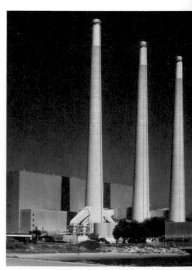

This oil-fired power station produces less sulfur dioxide emissions than a coal-fired power station.

Reducing emissions of nitrogen oxides

Most of the nitrogen oxides emitted come from car exhausts. We can reduce this by passing the exhaust gases through a **catalytic converter**. This removes the nitrogen oxides, converting them to harmless nitrogen gas.

Global warming

We have seen that although carbon dioxide in the air does make rain slightly acid, it is not really important in producing acid rain. However, it does have a harmful effect – it can contribute to **global warming**.

Carbon dioxide and the greenhouse effect

The Earth's atmosphere contains a very tiny proportion of carbon dioxide. Nearly 0.04% of the air is carbon dioxide. Although this is only a very small amount, it does have a very important and useful effect.

The carbon dioxide in the air acts like a blanket around the Earth. It helps to stop heat energy radiating from the Earth into space. Without any carbon dioxide in our atmosphere, the Earth would be much colder than it is now. It would be so cold that there probably would be no life on Earth at all.

This warming effect of the carbon dioxide is called the **greenhouse effect**. People often think that the greenhouse effect is bad, but, at the right level, it is not – it is really important for keeping the Earth warm so that animals and plants can live here.

Sun

Radiation from the Sun enters the Earth's atmosphere.

Some of the radiation is absorbed and is transformed into heat.

Carbon dioxide and other greenhouse gases stop the heat from escaping into space.

The heat warms the ground and atmosphere.

7 Describe one other important reason why living things rely on carbon dioxide in the atmosphere.

The problem with carbon dioxide is that the amount of it in the atmosphere is increasing, and the more of it there is, the more heat energy it traps. So the more carbon dioxide in the air, the warmer the Earth becomes. It is as though we were being wrapped up in a thicker blanket.

Before the Industrial Revolution, which happened in the 19th century, carbon dioxide made up about 0.027% of the air. Now it makes up 0.037%. This is thought to be because we have been burning more and more fossil fuels. The combustion of fossil fuels produces carbon dioxide.

There may be other reasons why the quantity of carbon dioxide in the air is increasing. We cannot be certain that it is all our fault, but most people think that we should try to reduce the quantity of carbon dioxide that we produce, which means burning less fossil fuel.

Why does it matter if the Earth is getting warmer? We cannot really predict exactly what will happen if it does, but things will certainly change. Some of the changes might seem pleasant – it might be enjoyable if we had warmer summers – but it is more likely that most of the changes would cause harm to living organisms and to human lives.

Warmer global temperatures might melt a lot of the ice that covers the Arctic and Antarctic. This would make sea levels rise, and low-lying land would be flooded by the sea, destroying many people's homes as well as wildlife habitats.

Weather patterns would change. In Britain we might expect more extreme storms and flooding in winter, and longer and more severe droughts in summer.

The centre of York was flooded by water from the River Ouse in November 2000. Was this a result of global warming, or would it have happened anyway? We will never know.

Venus

The planet Venus is a very similar size to Earth. Venus orbits the Sun at a distance of 108 million kilometres, and receives nearly twice as much radiation from the Sun as the Earth does.

Venus has a very thick atmosphere. The atmosphere is made almost entirely of carbon dioxide. In the upper layers, however, there are clouds of sulfuric acid droplets.

The dense atmosphere presses heavily down on to the surface of the planet. The pressure of the atmosphere at ground level is nearly 100 times greater than on Earth.

The thick atmosphere reflects sunlight very effectively. From Earth, this makes Venus look very bright. After the Sun and the Moon, it is the brightest object in the sky. You can see Venus through a telescope – it looks like a yellow disc – but unlike the Moon, you cannot see any features on its surface.

The surface of Venus is very hot, with an average temperature of about 460 °C. Surveys of the surface of Venus, made by a space probe, have shown that the rocks are mostly basalt, suggesting that there has been a lot of volcanic activity in the past.

a Explain why Venus 'receives nearly twice as much radiation from the Sun as the Earth does'.

b Give one other reason why the surface of Venus is so much hotter than Earth.

c There are are no rivers, lakes or seas on Venus. Explain why.

d If it did rain on Venus, what would you expect the pH of the rain to be? Explain your answer.

e Explain why the presence of basalt on Venus suggests there has been volcanic activity there in the past.

f Imagine you are in a spacecraft heading towards Venus, where you will be making the first landing by humans. What equipment are you taking with you to help you survive? What are you expecting it to be like when you get there?

Key ideas

Now that you have completed this chapter, you should know:

- how weathering, erosion and deposition help soil to form
- that rotting plant material is also an important part of soil
- how to measure the pH of soil
- that different kinds of plants grow best in soils with different pH values
- how farmers can alter the pH of soil
- what acid rain is, and how it is formed
- the effects of acid rain on living organisms, on rocks and on building materials
- how we can reduce the production of acid rain
- how carbon dioxide helps to keep the Earth warm
- how to weigh up some of the evidence that increasing carbon dioxide levels may be causing global warming.

Key words

acid rain	lime
calcium carbonate	manure
catalytic converter	nitrogen oxides
deposition	pioneer plants
emissions	soil
erosion	soil particles
global warming	sulfur dioxide
greenhouse effect	weathering
humus	

End of chapter questions

1 Find each of the words described below.

G	N	I	R	E	H	T	A	E	W	A	O
H	O	E	K	R	B	V	E	I	Y	L	P
U	I	E	N	O	T	S	E	M	I	L	N
M	T	Z	C	S	C	Y	T	S	A	E	O
U	A	S	O	I	L	W	B	N	R	N	I
S	R	R	M	O	T	J	T	R	E	I	T
K	I	X	Y	N	E	Y	U	T	E	L	S
P	P	R	O	X	I	F	L	L	V	A	U
M	S	S	W	I	L	J	I	A	P	K	B
C	E	E	R	U	N	A	M	S	T	L	M
D	R	F	S	Q	G	D	E	A	F	A	O
L	A	R	T	U	E	N	O	B	R	A	C

a This kind of converter helps to reduce emissions of nitrogen oxides from car exhausts.

b A substance made up of rock fragments and humus, in which plants grow.

c An igneous rock which forms when lava cools and solidifies above ground.

d The removal of rock fragments by water or the wind.

e The breakdown of solid rocks into small fragments, for example by water freezing in cracks, or by plant roots.

f Farmers may add this to soil to increase its pH.

g Farmers may add this to soil to reduce its pH.

h A word used to describe a solution with a pH more than 7.

i This dioxide is partly responsible for the greenhouse effect.

j This dioxide produces acid rain.

k This type of building stone is especially likely to be damaged by acid rain.

l Plant roots use oxygen from the air spaces in soil to carry out this process.

m The _____ of fossil fuels produces carbon dioxide.

n This kind of organism uses carbon dioxide from the air for photosynthesis.

o Dark, sticky material formed from rotting plants and animals which helps to hold soil particles together.

p A word used to describe a solution with a pH of 7.

2 These gases are found in unpolluted air.

nitrogen   oxygen   carbon dioxide   water vapour   argon

a Which of these gases are elements?
b Which of these gases are compounds?
c Which gas is found in the largest amount in the atmosphere?
d Which gas do all living organisms use for respiration?
e Which gas do plants use for photosynthesis?
f Which gas traps heat and so contributes to the greenhouse effect?
g Which two gases are produced when fossil fuels burn?
h Name one gas which is not in the list above, which can produce acid rain.

3 Chris tests the pH of six different samples of rain water. These are his results.

Sample	A	B	C	D	E	F
pH	5.5	5.2	4.8	4.2	5.6	4.5

a Suggest how Chris could find the pH of the samples of rain water.
b Which sample was the most acid?
c Which samples can be classed as 'acid rain'? Explain your answer.
d Explain why all the samples of rain water have a pH below 7.
e Suggest why some of the samples are more acid than others.

4 Make a poster about one of these:
• Acid rain
• Global warming.

12 Energy and electricity

When energy changes from one form to another, or is transferred from one place to another, things happen.

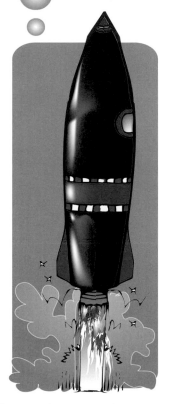

Chemical potential energy in the rocket fuel is changed into kinetic (movement) energy of the rocket, and also into sound energy and light energy.

As the switch is closed, electrical energy travels round the circuit and is changed into light energy and heat by the light bulb.

Chemical potential energy in the horse's muscles is changed into kinetic energy and then into gravitational potential energy (as the horse gets higher above the ground). The pole had gravitational potential energy when it was high up, and this is changed to kinetic energy as it falls, then to sound energy as it hits the ground.

We can see from these examples that during an energy transfer, energy never disappears. It just changes into a different form, or moves to a different place.

1 There is not much energy in the sound produced when the pole above hits the ground. What do you think happens to the rest of the energy that was in the falling pole?

In this chapter, we investigate some of the ways in which we can use energy changes to make things happen. We look particularly at electrical energy, because this is a really convenient kind of energy for doing all sorts of different useful things.

Electrical circuits

In Years 7 and 8 you studied electrical circuits and the symbols used when drawing circuits. This diagram shows those symbols and also includes the symbol for a voltmeter.

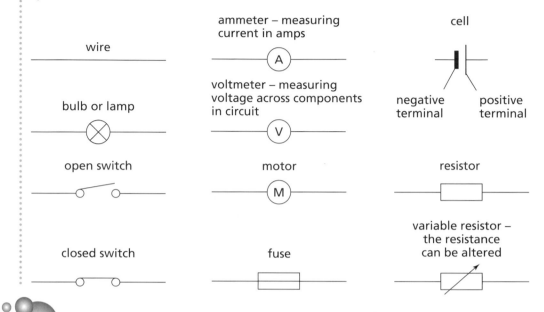

wire

ammeter – measuring current in amps

cell

negative terminal   positive terminal

bulb or lamp

voltmeter – measuring voltage across components in circuit

open switch

motor

resistor

closed switch

fuse

variable resistor – the resistance can be altered

Series and parallel circuits

These diagrams show a **series** circuit and a **parallel** circuit.

In a series circuit, there is only one pathway along which the current can travel.

In a parallel circuit, there is more than one pathway along which the current can travel.

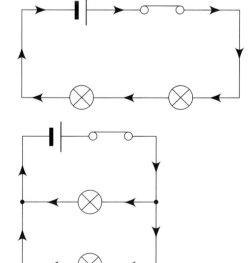

2 Draw a series circuit containing a cell, a bulb, a motor and a variable resistor.

3 Draw a parallel circuit that contains four different components and has at least three different pathways.

In a series circuit, the current flowing in the circuit is the same at every point in the circuit. It does not matter where you put your ammeter – it will always read exactly the same.

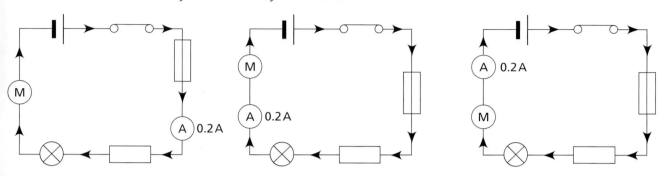

In a parallel circuit, the current splits up when it reaches a junction and follows different pathways. How much current flows along each pathway depends upon the components present. If the pathways are identical the same current will flow along each one.

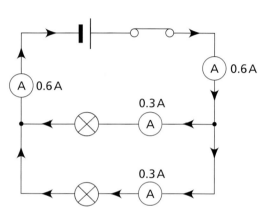

If the pathways are not identical, currents of different sizes may flow along each of them. The pathway that offers least resistance to the flow of current will have the largest current passing through it. The pathway with the largest resistance to the flow of current will have the smallest current passing through it.

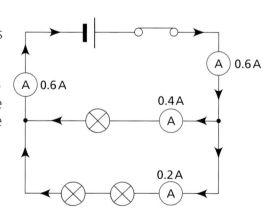

If we look carefully at the ammeters in these parallel circuits we can see that the sum of the currents in the different pathways is always equal to the current entering and leaving the cell.

YOU MAY BE ABLE TO DO WORKSHEET L2, 'CURRENT IN SERIES AND PARALLEL CIRCUITS'.

The current *returning* to the cell is exactly the same as the current that *left* the cell. Current is not used up.

4 What current will each of the numbered ammeters measure? All bulbs are identical.

a

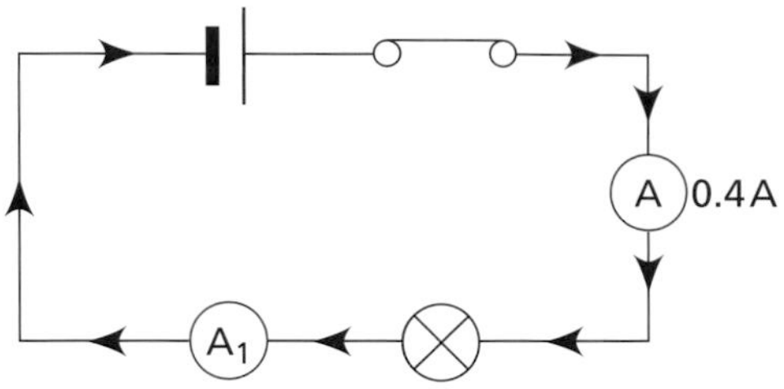

A) 0.4 A

A₁

b

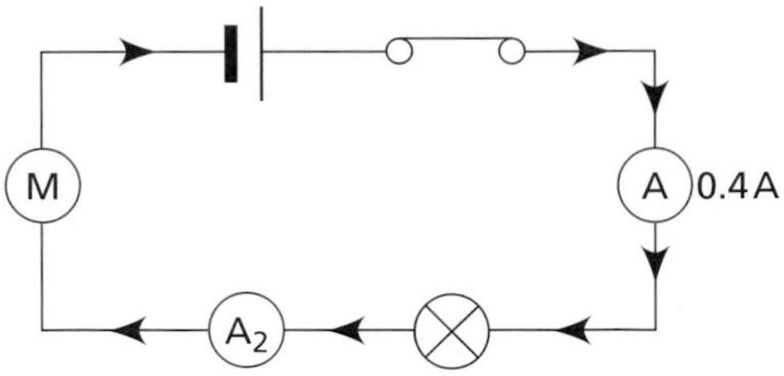

M

A) 0.4 A

A₂

c

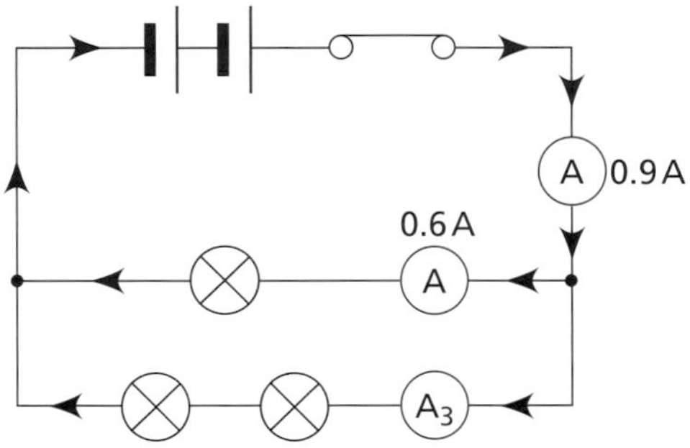

A) 0.9 A

0.6 A

A

A₃

d

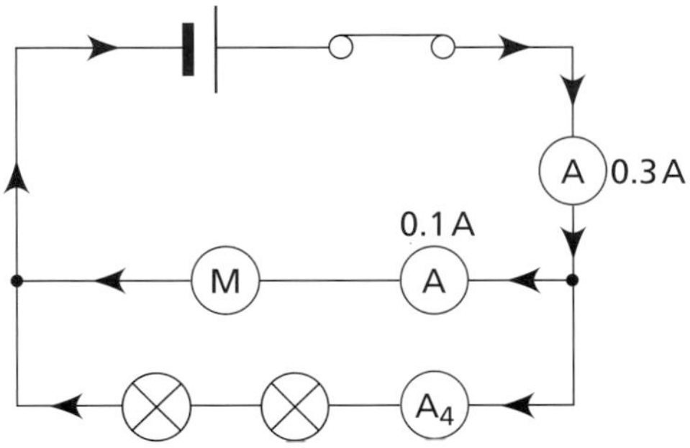

A) 0.3 A

0.1 A

M

A

A₄

e

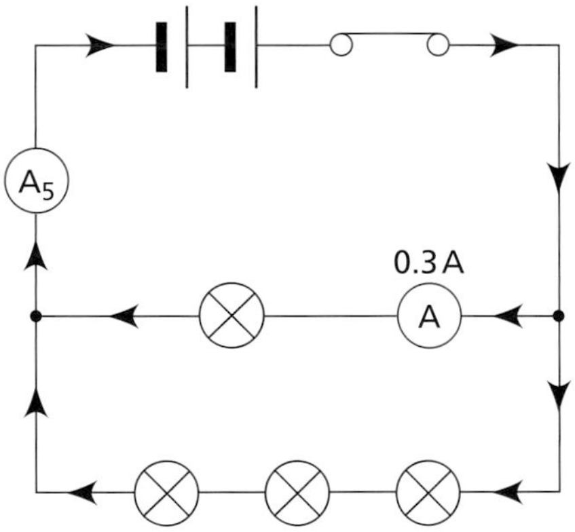

A₅

0.3 A

A

f

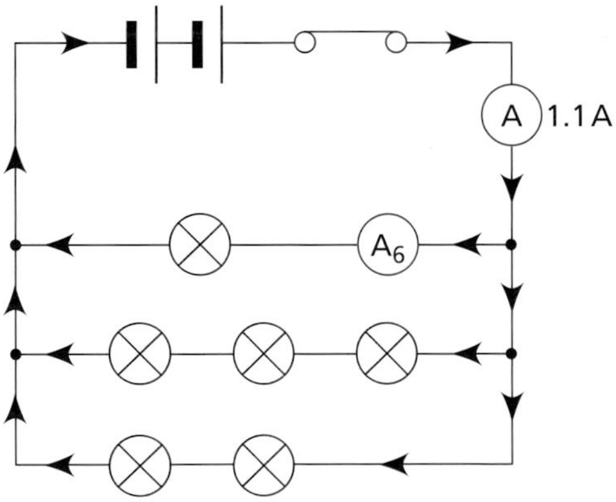

A) 1.1 A

A₆

Voltage

A cell 'pumps' current around a circuit. It gives the current energy, which the current then carries round the circuit.

The **voltage** of the cell is a measure of how much energy the current has been given. We can measure the voltage of a cell using a **voltmeter** connected across the terminals of the cell. Voltage is measured in units called **volts**. The abbreviation for volts is **V**.

This diagram shows where to connect the voltmeter to measure the voltage of a cell.

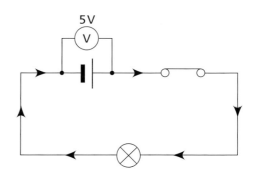

Measuring the voltage across a lamp

Although all the *current* returns to the cell when it has been round the circuit, not all the *energy* the current carries returns. As the electrical energy is carried round the circuit, it is changed into other forms of energy by the components in the circuit.

Connected across the terminals, we use a voltmeter to measure the energy that a cell is *giving* to the current in a circuit. We can also use a voltmeter to measure the amount of energy *changed* into other forms by components such as bulbs.

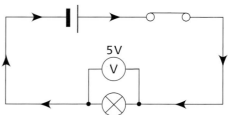

In the bulb, electrical energy from the circuit is changed into light energy and heat. We can connect a voltmeter across the bulb to measure the difference between the electrical energy on either side of the bulb. This shows how much energy is being transferred by the bulb.

5 Redraw this circuit to include:
 • an ammeter to measure the current flowing through the circuit
 • a voltmeter to measure the voltage across bulb A.

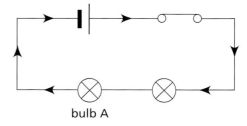

bulb A

6 Make a large copy of this circuit and include:
 • an ammeter to measure the current flowing through the cell
 • two more ammeters to measure the current flowing through each of the branches in the circuit
 • a voltmeter to measure the voltage across the cell
 • two more voltmeters to measure the voltage across each of the lamps.

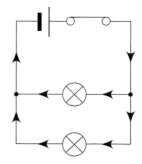

YOU MAY BE ABLE TO DO WORKSHEET L4, 'MEASURING VOLTAGE'.

Sharing out voltage in a circuit

As the current flows round a circuit, energy is shared between all the different components in the circuit.

In this circuit, the power supply has a voltage of 3 V.

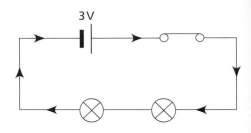

The two bulbs are identical, so each takes an equal share of the energy that the current is carrying. Thus each bulb has a voltage of 1.5 V.

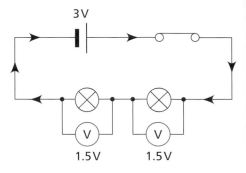

All the voltages across the components in a series circuit add up to the total voltage produced by the power supply.

7 What is the voltage across each bulb in this circuit?

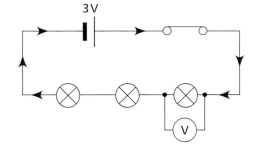

The energy in cells

Where does the energy provided by an electrical **cell** come from?

Cells contain chemicals and these chemicals store chemical potential energy. Inside the cell, the chemical potential energy is transformed into electrical energy.

A cell contains two **electrodes**. Sometimes, these are made of two different metals, and sometimes, one electrode is made of metal and the other is made of carbon. In most cells (batteries) that you can buy, one electrode is made of zinc and the other one is made of carbon. The electrodes are separated from each other either by a kind of paste (in a 'dry cell') or by a concentrated solution of an alkali (in an 'alkaline cell').

You may be able to do Worksheet L6, 'Fruit power'.

When you connect a cell into a circuit, its electrodes are connected to each other and a chemical reaction takes place inside the cell. During this reaction, chemical potential energy is changed into electrical energy. It is this electrical energy that the current carries round the circuit.

Cells and batteries

Technically speaking, many of the 'batteries' that you buy in shops are not really batteries at all – they are cells.

A cell is a device in which chemical potential energy is transformed into electrical energy. A **battery** is formed when two or more cells are connected together.

The cells you buy in shops have their voltages marked on them, and commonly used ones are 1.5 V. However, some of them have higher voltages than this. For example, PP9 batteries provide about 9 V.

If the device you want to run needs a higher voltage than one cell can provide, you can put two or more cells in series, to make a battery of cells. Connecting two 1.5 V cells together in series makes a battery with a voltage of 3 V.

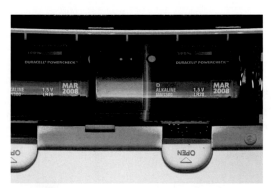

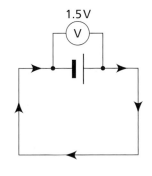

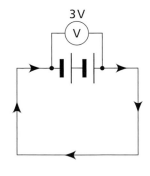

1.5 V

3 V

8 What voltage will you get if you put three 1.5 V cells together in series?

9 Why do you think it is important to put all cells the same way round?

High voltages

You would not receive much of an electric shock from a 1.5 V cell, or even from a 9 V one, but if you came into contact with the electricity supply to one of the sockets in your house, it would be a very different matter.

The electricity supply to your house and school has a voltage of 230 V. This means that the current flowing through the wires has a lot of energy and can be very dangerous if not used with care.

Even 230 V is low compared with the high voltages carried by overhead power lines and on railway tracks, where huge amounts of energy are involved.

Electricity is supplied to trains using this track by the live grey rail, which is slightly higher than the other two.

When electricity leaves a power station, its voltage may be as high as 400 000 V. To avoid danger to people, it is usually carried high above the ground through wires supported by tall pylons.

The high voltage is reduced to the domestic value by an electricity substation near your home.

Substations transform electricity from the high voltage used to send it over long distances to a lower voltage suitable for local distribution.

Generating electricity

Most of the electricity you use in your home does not come from cells – it comes from the mains supply, and this electricity is produced in power stations.

Generators

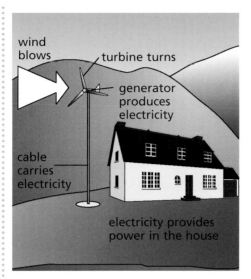

A **generator** is a device that produces electricity. It changes kinetic energy into electrical energy.

wind blows
turbine turns
generator produces electricity
cable carries electricity
electricity provides power in the house

Wind-powered generators can provide electricity for isolated homes.

Many bicycles have a simple kind of generator, called a **dynamo**. As the pedals are turned, the wheels go round and the movement of the wheels turns a magnet round inside a coil of wire. This produces an electrical current in the wire, and this current can be used to power the lights.

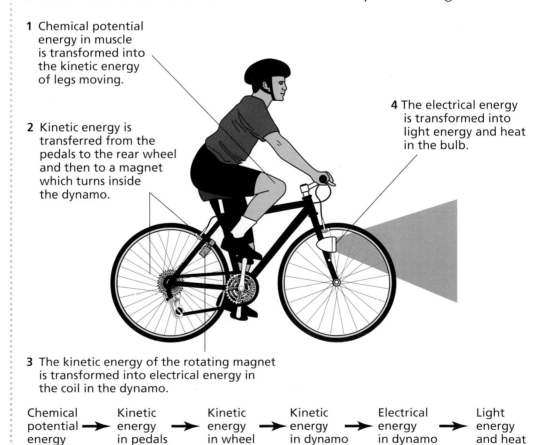

1 Chemical potential energy in muscle is transformed into the kinetic energy of legs moving.

2 Kinetic energy is transferred from the pedals to the rear wheel and then to a magnet which turns inside the dynamo.

4 The electrical energy is transformed into light energy and heat in the bulb.

3 The kinetic energy of the rotating magnet is transformed into electrical energy in the coil in the dynamo.

Chemical potential energy in muscle → Kinetic energy in pedals → Kinetic energy in wheel → Kinetic energy in dynamo → Electrical energy in dynamo → Light energy and heat in lamp

Power stations make electricity in a similar way. A large magnet is made to turn inside a coil and a current flows in the coil. The main difference between a power station and a bike dynamo is that everything is on a much bigger scale.

You would need a lot of people pedalling bikes to generate electricity on the scale of a power station.

In most power stations, a fuel is burnt and the heat energy it releases is used to boil water and produce steam, which is then passed through huge **turbines**. These turbines turn magnets inside large coils to generate electricity. The enormous quantities of energy involved mean that very high voltages are produced. A typical power station generates electricity at about 25 000 V.

This generator converts the kinetic energy of superheated steam into electricity. The steam produced by burning coal passes into a steam turbine to which this generator is connected.

Sources of energy

All kinds of different energy sources can be used for generating electricity. Provided that it can make a turbine turn, almost any source of energy will do.

◀ Anything that can produce heat energy – such as hot rocks deep below the ground, or burning fossil fuels, burning wood or other types of biomass, or using nuclear fuels – can be used to boil water and produce steam. This worker is checking the furnace of a coal-fired power station.

The kinetic energy of ▶ wind can be harnessed to turn wind turbines.

◀ Water falling downwards from a dam can turn turbines.

The kinetic energy of waves ▶ on the sea can be harnessed to turn turbines.

◀ The kinetic energy of water flowing in and out of a narrow channel with the tides can turn turbines.

10 Which of the sources of energy shown above are **renewable** sources?

Energy wastage

We use a great deal of energy in the devices in our homes, schools, workplaces and factories, and also for transport. The devices change one kind of energy into another kind, which does something useful for us.

For example, in a light bulb, electrical energy is changed into light energy. In a car, chemical potential energy in the petrol is changed into the kinetic energy of the car.

Unfortunately, quite a lot of the energy is usually changed into other forms as well – this is **wasted energy**.

Efficiency

Every time energy is transferred from one place to another, or transformed from one kind to another, some of it is wasted.

For example, if coal containing 1000 kJ is burnt in a steam engine, only 100 kJ of it is converted into kinetic energy. The other 900 kJ is changed into heat. This heat warms the engine, and escapes into the surroundings.

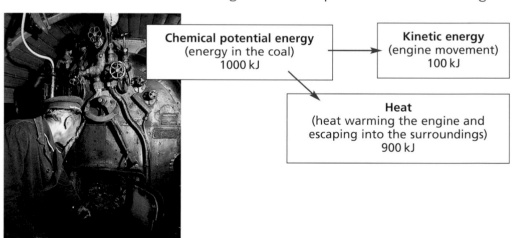

| Chemical potential energy (energy in the coal) 1000 kJ | → | Kinetic energy (engine movement) 100 kJ |
| | | Heat (heat warming the engine and escaping into the surroundings) 900 kJ |

When 100 J of electrical energy enters a light bulb, perhaps only 15 J of light energy is produced. The other 85 J is changed into heat. This warms the filament, the glass of the light bulb and the air around it.

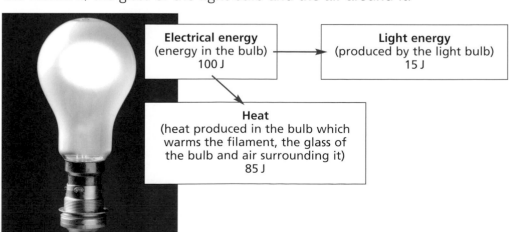

| Electrical energy (energy in the bulb) 100 J | → | Light energy (produced by the light bulb) 15 J |
| | | Heat (heat produced in the bulb which warms the filament, the glass of the bulb and air surrounding it) 85 J |

If we use energy-efficient light bulbs, we can improve on this. When 100 J of electrical energy enters an energy-efficient bulb, 60 J of light energy is produced.

11 How much energy is lost as heat from the energy-efficient light bulb?

When we say that a device is **efficient**, we mean that it does not waste very much energy. A lot of the energy that we put into it comes out in the form that we want.

12 Which of these devices is the most efficient? Which is the least efficient?

Device	Useful energy we get out for every 100 J we put in (J)
car petrol engine	30
car diesel engine	40
washing machine motor	70
gas-fired power station	50
steam engine	10

13 Sally uses a hair dryer on her wet hair. The hair dryer is very noisy.

    a What kind of energy is going into the hair dryer?

    b What two useful forms of energy is the hair dryer producing?

    c What unwanted form of energy is the hair dryer producing?

    d Draw a flow diagram to show the energy changes that are taking place.

Wind power for a village

In April 2003, the village of Pantperthog, near Machynlleth in Wales, became the first community in Britain to own and run its own wind turbine to generate electricity for the village.

Fifty-nine people in the village contributed to the cost of installing and setting up the wind turbine. The turbine is expected to produce enough electricity for everyone in the village, plus enough left over to sell to the nearby Centre for Alternative Technology, CAT. CAT has agreed to buy all the 'spare' electricity.

The turbine generates 75 kilowatts, which is enough power to provide electricity for 50 houses. It is 22 m high, with a diameter of 17.5 m. Everyone in the village helped to plan the project, and to install the turbine.

The villagers hope to make a profit on their investment, in addition to having free electricity. They are also hopeful that, by using the wind turbine, they are helping to reduce carbon dioxide emissions by as much as 70 tonnes per year. They feel that they are doing their bit towards slowing climate change.

a Explain how a wind turbine generates electricity.

b Explain why generating electricity using wind turbines might help to slow climate change.

c The installation of the wind turbine cost £81000. Many people in the village have each contributed at least £1000 towards it. How do they hope to get their money back?

d Not everyone likes the idea of a wind turbine near their house. What objections do you think people might have?

e Imagine that someone has had the idea of your community installing its own wind turbine. Decide whether or not you want this to happen, and then write a short talk that you could give at a local community meeting to decide whether or not to go ahead with the project.

Key ideas

Now that you have completed this chapter, you should know:

- that many devices we use involve energy changes
- terms used to describe different kinds of energy, such as kinetic, potential, light, chemical, heat and sound
- how to draw circuit diagrams using the correct symbols for all the components
- that a current carries electrical energy round a circuit
- that the current is not used up in the circuit, but the energy is transferred to the components in the circuit
- that the energy carried by the current is produced by an electrical cell
- how current behaves in series and parallel circuits
- how to measure the voltage of a cell or a component in a circuit
- that an electrical cell transforms chemical potential energy into electrical energy
- that dynamos and generators produce electricity by changing kinetic energy into electrical energy
- some examples of renewable sources of energy
- that in energy transfers some energy is always changed into unwanted forms.

Key words

battery	renewable
cell	series
dynamo	turbine
efficient	voltage
electrodes	voltmeter
generator	volts (V)
parallel	wasted energy

1 Copy and complete these sentences, using the following words. You can use each word once, more than once, or not at all.

> battery   chemical   potential   across   alongside   heat
> voltmeter   ammeter   resistor   series   parallel   current
> voltage   resistance

a Inside a cell, _____ _____ energy is changed into electrical energy. If the cell is connected in a complete circuit, a _____ carries the energy round the circuit.

b We can measure the voltage of a cell by connecting a _____ _____ it. If one cell does not provide enough voltage, we can connect two cells in _____ , producing a _____ of cells.

2 What energy changes are taking place?

a

b

c

d

e

3 This circuit contains two cells, three bulbs and a switch.

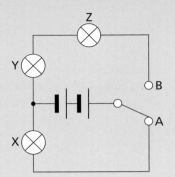

a Which bulb or bulbs are lit, with the switch in the position shown? Explain your answer.

b What will happen if the switch is moved to position B?

c Which bulb or bulbs will light up most brightly? Explain your answer.

d Redraw the circuit, adding:

- an ammeter to measure the current flowing through bulb X
- a voltmeter to measure the voltage across the cells.

e What energy changes are taking place in the cells when the switch is closed at either A or B?

f What energy changes are taking place in bulb X when the switch is in the position shown on the diagram?

4 Find out about two of these ways of generating electricity:

- using nuclear power
- using hot rocks
- using coal
- using water.

Write a very brief description of how the electricity is generated by each method. Then compare the ways in which each of your two chosen methods affects the environment.

5 Design a poster to warn children about the dangers of high voltages at an electricity substation, or on a railway.

Glossary and index

Carbon dioxide	A compound that contains carbon and oxygen. It has the formula CO_2. It is a colourless gas that plants combine with water in the process of photosynthesis to produce glucose. 102, 120
Carbon monoxide	A compound that contains carbon and oxygen and is a colourless gas. It has the formula CO, showing that each carbon atom is bound to only one oxygen atom (not two as in carbon dioxide). Carbon monoxide is very poisonous because it binds to haemoglobin, the oxygen-carrying protein in red blood cells, and prevents it from carrying oxygen. Carbon monoxide is formed during the incomplete combustion of substances that contain carbon atoms. 9, 103
Catalytic converter	An anti-pollution device fitted in car exhausts that uses a platinum catalyst. It changes carbon monoxide into carbon dioxide and water, and removes nitrogen oxides from the exhaust gases. 153
Cell (biological)	The smallest unit of a living organism. Most cells contain a nucleus, and all are surrounded by a cell membrane. 124
Cell (electrical)	A device in which chemical potential energy is transformed into electrical energy. A cell contains two electrodes. Either, these are made of two different metals, or, one electrode is made of a metal and the other is made of carbon. .. 164
Cellulose	The tough, fibrous material found in plant cell walls. 126
Centre of gravity	The point at which all the weight of an object is imagined to be concentrated.... 71
Chemical formula	A way of representing a chemical using letters and numbers. H_2O is the chemical formula for water and CO_2 is the chemical formula for carbon dioxide. 34
Chemical reaction	When elements or compounds combine to form a new material. 34
Chlorophyll	The green pigment that absorbs energy from sunlight. The energy is then used in photosynthesis. 121
Chloroplasts	Small parts in some plant cells. Chloroplasts contain lots of chlorophyll and are green. Photosynthesis takes place in chloroplasts. 121
Chromosome	A long piece of DNA which contains many genes. Humans have 46 chromosomes in the nucleus of each body cell. 78
Ciliated cell	A cell that has tiny, hair-like projections that move actively, pushing liquid and other material past them. Cells that line the airways and the oviducts are ciliated. 9
Clone	A group of genetically identical organisms. 85
Combustion	The process of burning. 102
Competition	Competition between organisms happens when they all need the same thing that is in short supply. For example, crop plants and weeds compete for water. 134
Compressible	Able to be squashed or made more compact. 68
Contraction	The shortening of muscles that brings about movement. Muscle contraction requires energy. 5
Copper sulfate	A compound that contains copper, sulfur and oxygen. It has the formula $CuSO_4$. 39, 54
Counterweight	A weight that exactly balances another weight. 73
Cow	A female bovine mammal. 83
DDT	A chemical pesticide that was widely used in the 1950s and 1960s before people realised that it harmed wildlife such as hawks and eagles. DDT is a persistent pesticide, meaning that it does not break down in the environment. It is now illegal to use DDT in Britain. 139
Decelerate	To slow down, to reduce speed. 25
Deficiency disease	A disease that occurs when the body does not get enough of a particular vitamin or mineral. The symptoms are different depending on which vitamin or mineral is in short supply. 11

Acknowledgements for photos

Every effort has been made to contact the holders of copyright material, but if any have been inadvertently overlooked, the publishers will be pleased to make the necessary arrangements at the first opportunity.

The publishers would like to thank the following for permission to reproduce photographs
(T = Top, B = Bottom, C = Centre, L= Left, R = Right):

Action Plus/Chris Barry, 17, Glyn Kirk, 27CR, Neil Tingle, 72R;
Dr John Butler, Armagh Observatory (http://star.arm.ac.uk), 21CR;
Martyn Chillmaid, 48C, 48B, 49B, 51, 53B, 166B, 170B, 171;
John Cleare/Mountain Camera, 63;
Corbis/Sandro Vannini, 49TR;
Ecoscene/John Liddiard, 121;
Energy Saving Trust/ecodyfi, 172;
Getty Images, 48T, 71;
Getty Images/Clive Mason, 4C, Robert Laberge, 4R, Adam Pretty, 4L, Darren England, 20T, Alex Livesey, 20BL, Clive Rose, 20CL, Agence Zoom, 22, David Taylor, 29, Mike Powell, 31;
Getty Images/Taxi/Phil Boorman, 21C;
Michael Holford, 49TL;
Holt Studios International/Nigel Cattlin, 81CL, 81B, 84, 137, Andy Burridge, 81TL, Wayne Hutchinson, 81CR;
Kit Houghton/Houghtonshorses, 81TR;
Sigurgeir Jonasson, 145;
Geoff Jones, 146, 147, 149, 165;
Andrew Lambert Photographic Collection, 39, 53T;
Lockheed Martin Aeronautics Company, 32;
Milepost 92½, 170C;
Military Picture Library/© William F. Bennett, 20BCR;
NASA, 90;
NHPA/Laurie Campbell, 27CL, ANT Photolibrary, 27BR, Daniel Heuclin, 151R;
National Motor Museum, 72L;
Rail Images, 166C;
Rex Features Ltd, 20BR, 21CL, 77;
The Roslin Institute, 85;
Science Photo Library/Biophoto Associates, 11, NASA, 26, 95T, 95R, 155, Klaus Guldrandsen, 44, Ron Church, 62, Alexis Rosenfeld, 74, Sheila Terry, 91, Victor Habbick Visions, 92, Chris Butler, 93, NASA/Goddard Space Flight Center, 94, Space Telescope Science Institute/NASA, 95L, Novosti, 101, Daniel Sambraus, 103, Damien Lovegrove, 108, Hank Morgan, 122B, Martin Bond, 127, 169BL, 169BR, Gordon Garradd, 150B, Simon Fraser, 151L, 152L, James Stevenson, 152R, Garry Watson, 154, US Department of Energy, 168, Sam Ogden, 169TL, Alan Sirulnikoff, 169CR, Alex Bartel, 169CL;
Self-Heating Can diagram supplied by the inventors, Dr Tony Rest and Dr Neil Richardson, Southampton University. Can manufactured by Thermotic Developments Ltd, 107;
SHOUT, 27BL;
Thermit Welding (GB) Ltd, 55;
C&S Thompson, 49C, 122T;
Tony Waltham Geophotos, 124.

Cover image: Laboratory glassware 'network', Getty Images/Paul Morrell

Published by HarperCollins*Publishers* Limited
77–85 Fulham Palace Road
Hammersmith
London
W6 8JB

Browse the complete collins catalogue at
www.collinseducation.com

10 9 8 7

ISBN-13 978-0-00-713587-5

British Library Cataloguing in Publication Data
A Catalogue record for this publication is available from the British Library

Commissioned by Martin Davies
Project coordinated by Pat Winter
Edited by Margaret Shepherd
Proofread and indexed by Linda Antoniw
Glossary prepared by Kathryn Senior
Photo research by Caroline Thompson
Design by AMR Ltd
Cover designed by Chi Leung
Illustrations by Art Construction, Phillip Burrows, Geoff Jones, David Woodroffe
Production by Sarah Robinson
Printed and bound by Printing Express, Hong Kong

Mixed Sources
Product group from well-managed
forests and other controlled sources
www.fsc.org Cert no. SW-COC-1806
© 1996 Forest Stewardship Council
FSC